ST. PAUL'S PARISH REGISTER

(STAFFORD -- KING GEORGE COUNTIES)

1715 - 1798

Compiled by
John Bailey Calvert Nicklin

CLEARFIELD

Originally published
1962

Reprinted for
Clearfield Company by
Genealogical Publishing Co.
Baltimore, Maryland
1990, 1994, 1995, 2005, 2007

ISBN-13: 978-0-8063-4591-8
ISBN-10: 0-8063-4591-8

Made in the United States of America

Stafford County was formed in 1664 from Westmoreland which had been formed in 1653 from Northumberland County which, in 1648, was taken from York. York County had been created in 1634 as Charles River and in 1642 the name was changed to York. The County of Stafford was named after the English county of the same name.

On May 27, 1664 the first County Court met and the following were present: Lt. Col. Robert Williams, Mr. Richard Heabord, Capt. John Alexander, Mr. Richard Fossaker, Mr. Roger Perfitt, Justices. Col. John Dodman was sworn in as Sheriff and Anthony Bridges was sworn in as Clerk of the County Court. On Sept. 7, 1664, William Green and Vincent Young were sworn wardens of Potomac Parish. On Nov. 28, 1664, Capt. John Alexander, Richard Fossaker, Robert Osborne, John Heabord, William Heabord, Robert Howson, Vincent Young, William Green, John Withers, Thomas Humphrey and Thomas Gregg composed the Vestry. Robert Osborne and John Withers were the Church Wardens. On April 3, 1667 "The Court doth order that the minister preach at three particular places in this county - viz: At the southeast side of Aquia and at the Court House and at Chotanck, at a house belonging to Robert Townshend; to officiate every Sabbath Day in one of these places successively until further Order." On June 12, 1667 Hugh Dodman, Henry Meese, George Mason, John Alexander, Richard Heabord, William Townshend, William Heabord, William Green, John Withers, Vincent Young and David Anderson were members of the Vestry. On July 25, 1680 a jury met at the house of "Mr. John Ashton." It was composed of the following: Joseph Hayward, Thomas Odonell, Burr Harrison, Robert Richards, Robert Alexander, William Key, Edward Humston, Jonah Randall, Anthony Buckner, William Banks, Samuel Hayward and Robert Hewitt. In 1680 Stafford County had two commit-tees, civil and military. On the former were: Col. George Mason, Major Andrew Gilson, Mr. James Ashton, Capt. Robert Massey, Mr. Malchi Peale, Mr. Vincent Young, Dr. William Banks, Mr. Anthony Buckner, Mr. Edward Thompson, Mr. Martin Scarlett and Mr. Matthew Thompson. On the latter committee were: Col. George Mason, Lt. Col. Cadwallader Jones, Major Andrew Gilson and Capt. Robert Massey.

Richmond County, Va. Order Book #4 dated Aug. 31, 1706 - Francis Thornton of St. Paul's Parish, Stafford county, to his daughter, Sarah, wife of Lawrence Taliaferro. On June 8, 1699 the following were listed: George Mason, sheriff; Robert Alexander, Matthew Thompson, Philip Buckner, John Harvey, and Rice Hooe, Quorum. Richard Fossaker, Joseph Sumner, William Williams, Thomas Owsley, John Waugh, Jr., John Washington, Edward Hart, Robert Colston and Thomas Gregg. On Dec. 22, 1691 a meeting of the Magis-trates and Militia Officers was held and there were present: Capt. Malachi Peale, Capt. John Withers, Mr. Edward Thomason (sic), Cornet William Downing, Capt. Martin Scarlett, Lieut. Charles Ellis, Ensigns Joseph Sumner and John West, Justices and Officers. Another meeting was held three months later (March 9, 1691/2) and the following Justices and Officers met: Capt. Malachi Peale, Capt. George Mason, Capt. John Withers, Mr. Matthew Thompson, Capt. Martin Scarlett, Mr. Philip Buckner, Mr. Robert Alexander, Mr. Richard Fossaker, Lieut. Sampson Darrell, Cornet William Downing, Ensign Joseph Sumner, Ensign Thomas Gilson, Ensign John West, Lieut. David Strahan of the Rangers.

On May 1, 1699 the following signed a petition: Robert Alexander, Edward Barton, Thomas Baxter, Giles Vandagasteel, John Waugh, Jr., John Simpson, David Straughan, G(eorge) Mason, Matthew Thompson, Richard Fossaker,

Philip Buckner, William Williams, John Washington, Robert Colston, Burr Harrison, Johnathon Mothershead, William Carpenter, Moses Linton, James Hansford (or Haverford), Giles Tillit, Thomas Watts, Richard Cole, Jo: Coal Jo: Mason, William Perkins, Frances Hackett, Thomas Prockter (sic), Thomas Stafford, Thomas Owsley, Thomas Collins, Hugh Burton and Thomas Norman.

On July 10, 1700 the following were signers of a petition: Robert Colson, William Williams, John Washington, Thomas Sumner, Edward Hart, William Fitzhugh, Jr., George Mason, Rice Hooe, Robert Alexander, Richard Fossaker, Charles Ellis, George Anderson, Samuel Burton, Thomas Harrison, Benjamin Colclough, John Colclough, John West and Matthew Thompson.

On Oct. 7, 1694 the following were Justices: Edward Thomason, John Withers, Matthew Thompson, Martin Scarlett, Edward Maddocks.

In 1700 William III, King of England, sent "Greetings" to George Maso Matthew Thompson, Robert Alexander, Rice Hooe, Joseph Sumner, John Waugh, J Edward Hart, Thomas Gregg, Richard Foote, Thomas Gilson, Philip Alexander, William Bunbury, Jr., John West and Charles Ellis, Gentlemen, and made them the Commission of the Peace for Stafford county. On Sept. 28, 1704, Coll. Rice Hooe, Lt. Col. William Fitzhugh, and Major Richard Fossaker were of th Militia; while Matthew Thompson, Joseph Sumner and Francis Thornton, Gentle men, were Justices. (Executive Journal of the Colonial Council, Vol. 2; pa 388). On Aug. 18, 1751 the Stafford County Officers were: William Fitzhug County Lieutenant; Henry Fitzhugh Jr., Colonel of Militia; Francis Thornton Lieutenant Colonel; William Fitzhugh, Major of Horse; Benjamin Strother, Major of Foot; Gerrard Fowke, first captain and Withers Conway, captain.

On Oct. 10, 1692 Philip Buckner was granted land in Chotanke (sic) Parish, Stafford county, beginning at Francis Dade's, adjoining John Willia Elizabeth Burnard, Christopher Boice, Hugh Dowdey and Jonas Revett.

Westmoreland county Wills & Deeds #2, pg. 151: April 29, 1698: Frances Howson and Charles Calvert, Gent., of Chotank Parish in ye county o Stafford

ST. PAUL'S PARISH

The first actual mention of the Parish which I have found is this abstract from the first Deed Book now extant of Stafford county: July 7, 1706- Margaret Hart of St. Paul's Parish, Stafford county, to Charles Asht of Washington Parish, Westmoreland county, for 150,500 acres of land, the said Ashton intending by the sufferences of God Almighty the said Margaret Hart to espouse, marry and take to wife. On July 10 "This deed recorded be tween Mrs. Margaret Hart and Coll. Charles Ashton, Gent." On Feb. 11, 1707 Rice Hooe of St. Paul's Parish sold land which had been granted to him and Thomas Gilson on Oct. 1, 1694, to Thomas Gilson, son and heir of the said Thomas.

About 1680 Potomac Parish was divided into two parishes, Overwharton and Chotanck (later St. Paul's). The Rev. John Waugh who had been minister of Potomac Parish as early as 1667 was in charge of the two new parishes until the end of the century. In 1699 he was elected a member of the House of Burgesses which refused to seat him because of his clerical capacity!

Col. William Fitzhugh, one of the most prominent residents of Stafford county in its early days, was baptized in St. Paul's Parish, Bedfordshire, England, on Jan. 10, 1651. It is highly probable that he named or was instrumental in naming the Virginia parish for that of his birthplace. There is in Hening a reference to John Withers, dec'd., of Stafford county, who in his lifetime was seized of a tract of land in the parish of St. Paul's, in the said county, called Chotanck, and by his will, dated Aug. 29, 1698, devised the same to his daughter Sarah. (Hening's Statutes, Vol. 6, pg. 513). This may mean that St. Paul's Parish was in existence as early as 1698. However, it is difficult to say whether or not the expression "called Chotanck" refers to the parish or to the land of Withers. Some of the first pages of the Parish Register are missing so it is impossible to tell just when it began. In the Virginia Magazine of History & Biography Vol. 1, pg. 377, there is a list of Virginia Parishes and under Stafford county, appears the following: 1702- Parishes- St. Paul's, tithes 346; Overwharton, tithes 518. Minister: John Frazier. In 1702 the Rev. John Frazier had become minister of St. Paul's. The Rev. Alexander Scott is usually given as the next minister, but in 1724 in his report to the Bishop of London, he states that he came to Virginia in 1711 and that he had "had no other church or parish but this" (ie., Overwharton of which he was at that time minister). And, as the Rev. David Stuart was Minister of St. Paul's at that time (1724), it is evident that the Rev. Alexander Scott cannot be included with the minister of St. Paul's Parish. The Rev. David Stuart served St. Paul's for 27 years, dying in 1749/50. He was succeeded by his son, The Rev. William Stuart, who served the Parish for almost half a century, dying in 1798 at the age of 75. During his term of service the present St. Paul's Church was constructed. The Parish Register, except for the first decade, was kept under the rectorship of the Stuarts, father and son. In 1777 the revision of the county lines threw St. Paul's Parish into King George County, where it has remained since that date. So for the first three score years the records in the Register are of Stafford county and for the last score of King George county.

One of the delightful personal items of the Parish is the record of the differences between the aristocratic (and doubtlessly dictatorial) Colonel William Fitzhugh and the indomitable "Parson" John Waugh. The Colonel and the Parson were continually at odds. The Colonel called the Parson "an egregious basser" and the Parson retorted by calling the Colonel a "Papist"! It has been said of the Parson that, like Job's war-horse, he could scent the battle from afar and so "smell out" more trouble and rush into it than any man of his time. He was constitutionally opposed to obeying the law about banns and licenses for marriage and ran a Gretna Green for runaway couples from Maryland. He was suspended during a period of six months and fined 10,000 pounds of tobacco, about 1674, for marrying a couple without banns or license. The last record of him at the beginning of the eighteenth century (1701) shows that he was convicted and suspended once more and apparently discharged from his parish. He was one of the instigators of the trouble in 1688 when the Northern Neck of Virginia was thrown into a turmoil by the rumor, started by the Parson, that the Roman Catholics in Maryland were planning to come over and conquer Stafford County, as well as Virginia, for King James. As a result he was arrested and imprisoned, the militia was called out and Colonel Fitzhugh complained that he "had to write above three quires of paper in an effort to check their pannick fears." He told the County Court in session in 1690/1 that he had come to Court to correct some of their erroneous actions, and refused to attend court again as a Justice until that body had reported the Parson's outrageous remarks to the Governor and Council.

In spite of the opinion of William Fitzhugh, Parson Waugh was a man of learning and wide political influence. He was a power in politics and finally succeeded in being elected a Burgess, although the House refused him his seat, as has been already stated. In or about 1701 he was succeeded as minister by the Rev. John Fraser who was in charge of both parishes until 1704. There is a gap between that date and the arrival of the Rev. David Stuart; however, the latter may have come over as early as 1715, after the Scottish Uprising for the Old Pretender, as he is said to have been a member, or at least a sympathizer, of the House of Stuart. It is said that a prominent member of the parish appealed to the Bishop of London to send a "sober, God-fearing man" as a minister of St. Paul's Parish and the result of this appeal was the sending of the Rev. David Stuart. I am indebted to the Rev. G. Maclaren Brydon, D. D., Treasurer of the Diocese of Virginia, for the notes regarding the controversy between the Rev. John Waugh and Col. William Fitzhugh and for other data of the parish.

Rev. John Waugh died in or before 1706 as his inventory was filed in that year.

VESTRYMEN OF ST. PAUL'S PARISH 1715-1798

Captain John Alexander, John Alexander, Jr., John Berryman (vice William Fitzhugh who moved from the Parish in 1771), Richard Bernard, Thomas Bunbury, Captain Baldwin Dade, Cadwallader Dade, Langhorne Dade, Townshend Dade (vice Samuel Washington who moved from the Parish in 1770), Colonel Henry Fitzhugh, Henry Fitzhugh, Jr., Henry Fitzhugh, Daniel Fitzhugh, William Fitzhugh, William Fitzhugh, Jr., Richard Foote, Gerard Fowke, Andrew Grant, Benjamin Grymes, John Hooe, William Hooe, Rice Wingfield Hooe, Charles Massey, Thomas Pratt, William Quarles, Thomas Short, Robert Stith, John Stith, William Storke, Charles Stuart, William Gibbons Stuart, John Stuart, Thomas Stribling (Lay reader), Francis Thornton, William Thornton, John Washington, Lawrence Washington, Samuel Washington, Robert Washington, Thomas Washington, John Waugh and Robert Yates. (All these names are found in the Parish Register). In a list of Vestrymen of Hanover Parish, King George county, the following names, which are to be found in St. Paul's Register, appear: Thomas Berry, Horatio Dade, Townshend Dade, Henry Fitzhugh Jr., Thomas Jett, Joseph Jones, Robert Stith, William Strother, William Thornton, John Washington, and Lawrence Washington, Sr. These names are listed for the period between 1723 and 1779.
In 1768 the following members were on the Vestry of the Parish: Capt. John Alexander, Capt. Baldwin Dade, Col. Henry Fitzhugh, Francis Thornton, John Washington, Samuel Washington and Lawrence Washington.

EXPLANATIONS

The following letters are used to indicate by abbreviations the datum used with each name in the Parish Register.

B.	Born
M.	Married

D.   Died
Bapt.   Baptised
OPR.   Overwharton Parish Register

The Julian Calendar was replaced with the Gregorian in 1582 by the suppression of the ten days which had accumulated, so to speak, since the Council of Nice in 325. In this way what should have been Oct. 5th became October 15th (1582). This adjustment of the days to the year became known as the Gregorian Calendar or the New Style. But the New Style Calendar, or the Gregorian, did not come into effect in England and her Colonies until 1752 when the eleven days were suppressed and Sept. 3rd became Sept. 14th, 1752. The act which authorized the new method of reckoning time in 1752 shortened the preceding year by almost three months. Until that time the new year began on the Feast of the Annunciation (Our Lady's Day), March 25th. The year 1751 was the last to begin on March 25th. From 1751 onward the years began, as today, with January 1st. Prior to March 25, 1751 the days of the first three months of the year, ending with March 24th were customarily written doubly, if I may put it that way, by using the last numeral of the year soon to end and also the last numeral of the succeeding year. Thus Jan. 1, 1750/1 was the correct way of writing the date of the year 1750 which did not end until March 24th at midnight. March 24, 1750/1 was succeeded by March 25, 1751, the year from that time onward becoming simply 1751 et seq. This year ending on Dec. 31, 1751 and for the first time a new year began on Jan. 1st in England and her Colonies. Jan. 1, 1752 began the New Style Calendar as such. A good example of this double-dating is this: George Washington was born on Feb. 11, 1731/2 (Old Style, often written simple O.S.), but when the New Style (or N.S.) came into effect in 1752, the suppression of eleven days also became effective and changed the date to Feb. 22. He himself authorized the changed birthdate and Feb. 22 assumed its great significance to Americans before his death at Mt. Vernon on December 14, 1799.

It must be borne in mind that the original Register is not complete, is in bad shape and on some pages quite illegible. Every effort has been made to decipher as many entries as possible and a great deal of success has been achieved fortunately. It is impossible to say how many pages are now missing, but perhaps as many as ten pages are lost at the beginning of the Register. Otherwise it seems complete but of course there must be pages missing from the earlier parts of the book, due to its great age, here and there. Two fragments are available but incomplete and without a date (ie, the year), parts of pages. All references to the slaves have been omitted from this arrangement of the Parish Register.

Raised numerals in the text refer to notes at the end of this volume.

A

M. John Acres and Dully Griffin, May 28, 1790.
M. Mary Adams and George Elliott, April 26, 1728.
D. William Adams, Oct. 28, 1735.
B. Frances Anne, dau. of Jane Adderton, Sept. 5, 1735.
M. Thomas Adams and Katherine Skinner, Oct. 18, 1738.
M. John Addison and Mary Ann Fingleston, April 17, 1761.[1]
B. Anne, dau. of John and Mary Anne Addison, Feb. 4, 1762.
B. William, son of John and Mary Ann Addison, June 5, 1765.
B. Verlinda, dau. of John and Mary Anne Addison, Oct. 8, 1764.
B. Sarah, dau. of John and Mary Anne Addison, Aug. 13, 1767.
B. James, son of John and Mary Anne Addison, July 6, 1769.
M. Margaret Addison and John Sweeny, Oct. 6, 1769.
M. John Addison and Monica Bryant, March 19, 1789.
M. Sarah Addison and John Watson, Feb. 27, 1790.
D. Elizabeth Adrington, Dec. 4, 1725.
D. Francis Adrington, Dec. 4, 1725.
D. Helen Aisom, April 2, 1726.
M. Philip Alexander and Sarah Hooe, Nov. 11, 1726.
M. Anne Alexander and John Hoe, Nov. 23, 1726.
B. Frances, dau. of Philip and Sarah Alexander, Oct. 5, 1728.
B. Jane, dau. of Philip and Sarah Alexander, Jan. 12, 1729/30.
B. Elizabeth, dau. of Philip and Sarah Alexander, Dec. 24, 1731.
M. Parthenia Alexander and Dade Massey, Jr., Jan. 17, 1731/2.
B. Sarah, dau. of Philip and Sarah Alexander, Sept. 30, 1733.
M. John Alexander and Susanna Pearson, Dec. 15, 1734.
D. Major Robert Alexander, Oct. 5, 1735.
B. John, son of Philip and Sarah Alexander, Nov. 13, 1735.
D. Elizabeth Alexander, March 23, 1735/6.
M. Sarah Alexander and Baldwin Dade, Aug. 7, 1736.
B. Charles, son of John and Susanna Alexander, July 20, 1737.
D. Mrs. Anne Alexander, Sept. 23, 1739.
B. John, son of John and Susanna Alexander, Jan. 15, 1739/40.
B. Philip, son of Philip and Sarah Alexander, May 31, 1741.
B. Anne, dau. of John and Susanna Alexander, Feb. 9, 1741/2.
B. William, son of Capt. Philip and Sarah Alexander, Mar. 3, 1743/4.
B. Susanna, dau. of John and Susanna Alexander, Apr. 12, 1744.
B. Gerard, son of John and Susanna Alexander, June 13, 1746.
B. Robert, son of Philip and Sarah Alexander, Aug. 2, 1746.
B. Simon Pearson, son of Capt. John and Susanna Alexander, Jan. 20, 1747/8.
M. Jane Alexander and Henry Ashton, Feb. 23, 1748/9.
M. Frances Alexander and John Stuart, Feb. 16, 1749/50.
M. Sarah Alexander and John Fendall, Sept. 24, 1751.
B. Mary, dau. of John and Lucy Alexander, Nov. 26, 1756.
B. Lucy, dau. of John and Lucy Alexander, Dec. 4, 1757.
B. William, son of John and Susanna Alexander, Apr. 29, 1758.
B. Sarah, dau. of John and Lucy Alexander, Nov. 17, 1758.
M. Anne Alexander and Charles Binns, Oct. 4, 1759.
B. Philip Thornton, son of John and Lucy Alexander, Oct. 14, 1760.
B. Frances, dau. of John and Lucy Alexander, Aug. 24, 1762.
B. Alice, dau. of John and Lucy Alexander, June 20, 1764.
M. William Alexander and Sigismunda Mary Massey, Apr. 18, 1765.
M. Susanna Alexander and Pearson Chapman, July 31, 1766.
B. William Thornton, son of John and Lucy Alexander, June 28, 1768.
M. Mary Alexander and George Thornton, Oct. 9, 1773.

M. Lucy Alexander and John Taliaferro, Jan. 24, 1774.
M. Sarah Alexander and Seymour Hooe, Mar. 9, 1776.
M. Lucy Alexander and William Quarles, Oct. 20, 1784.
B. Anne, dau. of Archibald and Sarah Allen, Dec. 17, 1717.[2]
D. James Allen, Apr. 11, 1720.
B. Mary, dau. of Archibald and Sarah Allen, Oct. 2, 1721.
D. Sarah, wife of Archibald Allen, Nov. 12, 1721.
M. Archibald Allen and Penelope Skinner, Dec. 26, 1722.
D. John Allen, Oct. 14, 1725.
M. Francis Allen and Katherine Campbell, Nov. 17, 1747.
M. Andrew Allen and Alice Sebastian, Feb. 12, 1750/1.
M. Richard Allen and Nancy Jones, Feb. 4, 1788.
M. John Allenthrope and Anne Sebastian, Apr. 16, 1723.
B. Anne, dau. of John and Anne Allenthrope, Dec. 7, 1725.[3]
B. Sarah, dau. of John and Anne Allenthrope, Apr. 2, 1728.
B. John, son of John and Anne Allenthrope, June 3, 1732.
B. Elizabeth, dau. of John and Elizabeth Allenthrope, Apr. 10, 1735.
B. Mildred, dau. of John and Mary Allenthrope, June 8, 1738.
M. Anne Allenthrope and John Smith, Mar. 7, 1748/9.
M. Jane Allerton and Robert Reddish, Oct. 12, 1735.
B. Henry, son of Moses and Anne Allgood, Mar. 23, 1774.
M. William Allison and Anne Fitzhugh, Nov. 21, 1740.
B. Mary Anne, dau. of William and Anne Allison, Oct. 17, 1741.
B. John, son of William and Anne Allison, Jan. 21, 1742/3.
B. William, son of Dr. William and Anne Allison, June 6, 1744.
B. Henry, son of William and Anne Allison, Sept. 10, 1745.
D. Mary Anne, dau. of Dr. William Allison, Jan. 5, 1746/7.
D. Henry, son of Dr. William Allison, July 5, 1747.
M. William Allison and Anne Hooe, June 26, 1772.
M. John Alsop and Mary McDonald, Aug. 20, 1737.
B. Edward, son of John and Mary Alsop, Jan. 13, 1737/8.
M. John Alsop and Elizabeth Conway, Dec. 30, 1739.
B. Mary, dau. of John and Elizabeth Alsop, Mar. 26, 1741.
B. Elizabeth, dau. of John and Elizabeth Alsop, Mar. 8, 1743/4.
B. Sarah, dau. of John and Elizabeth Alsop, June 17, 1747.
M. Elizabeth Alsop and William Jones, Feb. 9, 1749/50.
M. Elizabeth Alsop and John Barrett, May 25, 1760.
M. Robert Alsop and Elizabeth Mardus, Jan. 3, 1791.
B. Thomas, son of William and Anne Ambrose, Oct. 15, 1731.
M. Thomas Ammon and Sarah Edrington of Sittingbourne Parish, Jan. 24, 1733/4.[4]
M. Mary Ancrum and John Smith, Feb. 17, 1717/8.
M. John Ancrum and Mary Thomas, Jan. 27, 1726/7.
M. Mary Ancrum and John Taylor, Feb. 27, 1726/7.
B. Sarah, dau. of John and Mary Ancrum, Nov. 23, 1727.[5]
B. Katherine, dau. of John and Elizabeth Ancrum, Sept. 30, 1731.
B. Frances, dau. of John and Mary Ancrum, Feb. 3, 1733/4.
M. William Ancrum and Margaret Colvin, Dec. 24, 1734.
D. William Ancrum, Jan. 6, 1734/5.
D. John Ancrum, Jan. 1, 1735/6. (1734/5?)
B. John, son of John and Mary Ancrum, Aug. 3, 1736.
D. John Ancrum, Jan. 12, 1736/7.
M. Mary Ancrum and George Bush, Nov. 14, 1737.
M. Joel Ancrum (Anchorom?) and Verlinda Settle, Sept. 12, 1745.
M. Sarah Ancrum and Thomas Hawkins, July 13, 1746.
M. Mary Anderson and Martin Frayn, July 9, 1758.
M. William Ashmore and Nancy Edrington, Jan. 14, 1781.
M. Elizabeth Armour and James Thomson, Aug. 10, 1724.

M. George Arnold and Sarah White of King George Co., Nov. 9, 1758.
M. Jemima Arnold and John Clift, Dec. 26, 1777.
M. Charles Ashton of Washington Parish and Sarah Butler of this Parish, Sept. 22, 1733.
M. Henry Ashton and Jane Alexander, Feb. 23, 1748/9.
M. Mary Ashton and Jacob Wray, May 13, 1761.
M. John Ashton and Elizabeth Jackson, May 16, 1766.
M. Lawrence Ashton and Elizabeth Ashton, Apr. 19, 1768.
M. Lawrence Ashton and Hannah Gibbons Dade, Feb. 1, 1779.
M. Mary Watts Ashton and John Waugh, Nov. 4, 1790.
B. Susannah, dau. of Philip and Mary Atkinson, Sept. 27, 1715.
D. Philip Atkinson, Jan. 12, 1735/6.
B. Richard, son of Samuel and Mary Atwell, Nov. 27, 1763.
B. Samuel, son of Samuel and Mary Atwell, June 16, 1766.
B. Francis, son of Samuel and Mary Atwell, May 19, 1768.
M. Mary Atwell and Thomas Moss, Sept. 10, 1772.
B. Elizabeth, dau. of William and Anne Awbry, Feb. 6, 1733/4.
D. William Awbry, Apr. 2, 1736.
B. Frances, dau. of William and Anne Awbry, Mar. 3, 1735/6.
M. Anne Awbry and John Sevier, June 1, 1738.[6]
M. Sarah Awbry and William Garrett, Feb. 4, 1741/2.

B

M. Sarah Bagjob (?) and Jethro Burnsplat, Oct. 21, 1729.
M. John Bailey and Sarah Frank, Jan. 6, 1745/6.
M. John Baker and Sarah Walker, Oct. 30, 1725.
B. Thomas, son of John and Sarah Baker, Jan. 19, 1726/7.
D. John Baker, June 26, 1728.
M. Winifred Baker of Westmoreland and William Strother, Sept. 26, 1765.
M. Benjamin Baker and Mildred Berry, Nov. 10, 1791.
M. Anne Balb (Ball?) and John Smith, Dec. 26, 1765.
B. Benjamin, son of Benjamin and Anne Ball, Sept. 13, 1742.
B. Anne, dau. of Benjamin and Anne Ball, July 17, 1745.
B. Elizabeth, dau. of Benjamin and Anne Ball, Oct. 4, 1747.
B. Susannah, dau. of Benjamin and Anne Ball, Aug. 28, 1752.
B. James, son of Benjamin and Anne Ball, Apr. 7, 1755.
D. William Balltrop, Mar. 1, 1719/20.[7]
B. Nelly, dau. of Elizabeth and William Bankhead, May 15, 1777.
M. Robert Barber and Penelope Gorman, Oct. 26, 1747.
M. James Barber and Susanna Dickerson, Sept. 25, 1779.
M. Elizabeth Barker and John MacClanin, Mar. 24, 1793.
B. Henry, son of Henry and Elizabeth Barnes, Oct. 12, 1740.
B. William, son of Rehobeth and Julia Barnfather, May 19, 1717.
M. Frances Barnfather and John Wells, June 18, 1723.
M. Rehobeth Barnfather and Elizabeth Regg, Dec. 31, 1724.
M. Edward Barradoll and Sarah Fitzhugh, Jan. 5, 1735/6.
B. Margaret & Helen, daus. of Richard and Margaret Barrett, Apr. 19, 1728.
B. William, son of Richard and Joyce Barrett, Aug. 20, 1734.
B. Richard, son of Richard and Joyce Barrett, Mar. 19, 1737/8.
B. Anne, dau. of Elizabeth Barrett, Nov. 18, 1740.
B. Mary, dau. of Richard and Joyce Barrett, Sept. 21, 1741.
M. Joyce Barrett and Joseph Clift, June 22, 1743.
M. Thomas Lewis Barrett and Hester Stripling, Apr. 16, 1744.
B. Keturah, dau. of Sarah Barrett, Nov. 18, 1746.
M. John Barrett and Elizabeth Alsop, May 25, 1760.

B. Richard, son of John and Elizabeth Barrett, Feb. 9, 1764.
B. Anne Conway, dau. of John and Elizabeth Barrett, May 16, 1766.
B. John, son of John and Elizabeth Barrett, Mar. 9, 1768.
M. William Barrett and Mary Hudson, Dec. 30, 1785.
M. Mary Barron and Joseph Hall, Oct. 13, 1727.
M. Timothy Barrington and Mary Robbins, Oct. 15, 1731.
B. Alse, dau. of John and Mary Barton, June 20, 1716.
B. William, son of William and Anne Barton, Dec. 25, 1725.
M. William Barton and Sarah Hamm, Dec. 1, 1730.
B. Elizabeth, dau. of William and Sarah Barton, Dec. 20, 1731.
B. John, son of William and Sarah Barton, Mar. 10, 1733/4.
B. John, son of John and Christina Bastin, Apr. 11, 1751.
M. John Bateman and Anne Williams, Feb. 4, 1740/1.
M. Anne Bateman and John Limit, Apr. 6, 1751.
M. Thomas Bateman and Winifred Kelly, Feb. 7, 1771.
B. Reuben, son of James and (Sarah) Bates, Jan. 24, 1730/1.
M. Reuben Bates and Sarah Prestridge, Dec. 4, 1757.
B. William, son of Reuben and Sarah Bates, Oct. 3, 1764.
D. Thomas Baxter, May 6, 1722.
B. Anne, dau. of Abraham and Mary Baxter, Jan. 2, 1725/6.
D. Frances Baxter, Jan. 23, 1725/6.
D. Abraham Baxter, Apr. 19, 1726.
M. William Baxter and Mary Rawlings, Apr. 1, 1735.
B. Peggy, dau. of William and Mary Baxter, Mar. 29, 1740.
M. Anne Baxter of this Parish and Thomas Butler of Washington Parish, Sept.
   22, 1742.
B. John, son of William and Mary Baxter, Dec. 16, 1742.
M. Mary Baxter and William Jones, July 26, 1744.
B. Nathaniel, son of William and Mary Baxter, July 24, 1745.
M. James Baxter and Sarah Sims, Oct. 20, 1764.
M. James Baxter and Anne Brisse, June 7, 1767.
B. James, son of James and Anne Baxter, Oct. 2, 1769.
M. Mary Beach and John Clift, July 2, 1745.
M. Anne Beach and Solomon Hardwick, Sept. 25, 1748.
M. Bethethland Beach and James Scribner, Nov. 7, 1773.
D. John Beal, Nov. 26, 1731.
M. John Beattie and Anne Whiting, Sept. 10, 1779.
M. Daniel Beattie and Susannah Rogers, Aug. 2, 1781.
M. John Bedford and Margaret Golding, Aug. 8, 1729.
M. Christopher Bell and Alice Proudlove, June 4, 1726.
M. Eleanor Bell and John McLean, Apr. 14, 1745.
D. Elizabeth Bennett, May 26, 1718.
M. Lucy Bennett and John Ross, Oct. 14, 1731.
M. Richard Bennett and Joyce Duncomb, Sept. 21, 1729.
M. James Bennett and Elizabeth Hubbard, Dec. 1, 1731.
B. Moses, son of James and Elizabeth Bennett, Dec. 22, 1732.
B. Barbara, dau. of James and Elizabeth Bennett, Nov. 20, 1737.
B. Behethland, dau. of James and Elizabeth Bennett, Feb. 15, 1739/40.
M. Cossum Bennett and Katherine Bunbury, Jan. 7, 1742/3.
B. Charles Ellis, son of Cossum and Katherine Bennett, Aug. 23, 1752.
M. Thomas Bennett (?) and Mary Horsey, June 18, 1758.
M. Jannet Bennett and James Seaton Ryan, Apr. 5, 1763.
M. Behethland Bennett and Hezekiah Kirk, Feb. 10, 1778.
M. William Bennett and Mary Johnson, Nov. 9, 1782.
B. William, son of Charles and Judith Benson, Feb. 10, 1750/1.
M. William Bentley and Jane Bussey, Mar. 14, 1768.

M. Richard Bernard and Elizabeth Storke, Aug. 29, 1729.
B. Richard, son of Richard and Elizabeth Bernard, Sept. 20, 1734.
B. John, son of Richard and Elizabeth Bernard, Dec. 29, 1735.
M. William Bernard and Winifred Thornton, Nov. 25, 1750.
B. Grace, dau. of James and Sarah Berry, Jan. 16, 1719/20.
B. Frances, dau. of Joseph and Catherine Berry, Nov. 11, 1721.
B. Joseph, son of Joseph and Catherine Berry, Apr. 27, 1723.
M. James Berry and Grace Powell, May 28, 1723.
D. Margaret, dau. of Joseph and Catherine Berry, July 16, 1725.
B. Benjamin, son of Joseph and Catherine Berry, Oct. 16, 1724.
B. Sarah, dau. of James and Grace Berry, Jan. 15, 1726/7.
B. Margaret, dau. of Joseph and Catherine Berry, June 14, 1726.[8]
M. Enoch Berry and Dulcibella Bunbury, December 12, 1726.
M. Margaret Berry and Thomas Kelton, Dec. 24, 1726.
D. Sarah Berry, Nov. 16, 1729.
D. Jane Berry, a child, Dec. 1, 1729.
B. William, son of James and Grace Berry, Feb. 23, 1731/2.
B. Grace, dau. of James and Grace Berry, Feb. 4, 1733/4.
B. Elizabeth, dau. of James and Grace Berry, June 6, 1735.
B. Marmaduke and Virginia Palmer, son and dau. of James and Grace Berry,
   Jan. 3, 1737/8.
D. James Berry, Jan. 6, 1738/9.
M. Frances Berry and Thomas Golding, Jan. 28, 1738/9.
M. Anne Berry and Samuel Jackson, Feb. 10, 1739/40.
B. Anthony, son of Grace Berry, June 28, 1744.
M. James Berry and Elizabeth Griffin, Aug. 19, 1747.
M. Thomas Berry and Elizabeth Washington, Nov. 19, 1758.
M. Thomas Berry and Sarah Gardiner, Oct. 21, 1784.
M. Mildred Berry and Benjamin Baker, Nov. 10, 1791.
M. Enoch Berry and Judith Fowke, Nov. 23, 1791.
M. Rose Berryman of King George and Richard Taliaferro of Essex, June 10,
   1726.
M. Behethland Berryman and Thomas Booth, Oct. 10, 1727.
M. Frances Berryman of Washington Parish and George Foote of this Parish,
   Dec. 3, 1731.
B. John, son of Gilson and Hannah Berryman, June 23, 1742.
M. William Berryman and Rebecca Vowles, Sept. 10, 1743.
B. Behethland, dau. of Gilson and Hannah Berryman, Mar. 23, 1743/4.
B. Andrew Gilson, son of Gilson and Hannah Berryman, June 3, 1745, and
   baptized June 8, 1745.
B. Rose, dau. of Gilson and Rose Berryman, Dec. 28, 1747.
D. Gilson Berryman, Gentleman, Apr. 4, 1749.
M. Sarah Berryman and Cadwallader Dade, Aug. 20, 1752.
M. Behethland Gilson Berryman and John Thornton, Dec. 13, 1761.
B. Gilson Newton, son of John and Martha Berryman, Mar. 20, 1762.
B. Andrew Gilson, son of John and Martha Berryman, Apr. 15, 1764.
B. Hannah, dau. of John and Martha Berryman, Apr. 21, 1766.
B. Sarah Foote, dau. of John and Martha Berryman, Oct. 21, 1768.
B. Millie, dau. of Henry and Mollie Besley, Apr. 28, 1747.
M. Margaret Bignell and Michael Kenny, July 29, 1750.
D. John Bingham, a servant of John Mealy, Sept. 4, 1717.
M. Charles Binns and Anne Alexander, Oct. 4, 1759.
M. Justinian Birch and Behethland Dade, June 30, 1777.
M. Peggy Birch and Samuel Johnson, July 28, 1785.
M. Elizabeth Bishop and George Tavernor, Jan. 2, 1739/40.
M. Michael Black and Sarah Radford, Dec. 3, 1752.

M. Theodorick Bland and Sarah Fitzhugh, Dec. 5, 1772.
B. John, son of Theodorick and Sarah Bland, Apr. 1, 1774.
M. Elizabeth Blakeman and Henry Locke, Feb. 6, 1724/5.
M. George Blankenship and Jane Butler, Feb. 12, 1739/40.
B. Arthur, son of George and Jane Blankenship, Sept. 16, 1743.
M. Jane Blankenship and Nathaniel Price, July 25, 1746.
M. John Blaxton and Mary Dade, Oct. 10, 1777.
M. Margaret Bolling and John Franklin, Aug. 18, 1716.
M. Elizabeth Bolling and John Thornberry, Dec. 14, 1749.
M. Priscilla Bolling and Thomas Phillips, Apr. 13, 1760.
B. William, son of Jesse and Sarah Bolling, June 1, 1772.
M. Elizabeth Bolling and Robert Clift, Jan. 21, 1777.
M. Eleanor Bolton and William Long, May 15, 1749.
M. Thomas Booth and Behethland Berryman, Oct. 10, 1727.
D. Behethland Booth, Oct. 9, 1728.
M. James Boswell and Mary Stuart, Apr. 6, 1744.
B. Mary, dau. of James and Mary Boswell, Mar. 13, 1744/5.
B. James and Thomas sons of James and Mary Boswell, Oct. 24, 1747.
M. Mary Boswell and David Jones, Feb. 18, 1763.
D. Anne, dau. of Daniel and Frances Bourn, Aug. 1, 1718.
B. Elizabeth, dau. of Daniel and Frances Bourn, Jan. 1, 1721/2.
B. Anne, dau. of Daniel and Frances Bourn, Oct. 2, 1725.
D. Frances Bourn, Oct. 23, 1731.
M. James P. Bowie and Mary Anne Bradshaw, Sept. 16, 1788.
M. Elizabeth Bowin and William Skidmore, May 11, 1747.
M. Simon Bowling and Anne Newton, Dec. 5, 1722.
B. John, son of William and Elizabeth (Bowling?) --1729.
B. Elizabeth, dau. of William and Eleanor Bowling, Apr. 28, 1725.
M. Benjamin Bowling and Mary Latham, July 27, 1725.
M. William Bowling and Sarah Kirk, June 24, 1726.
M. William Bowling and Elizabeth Kidwell, Sept. 7, 1726.
M. Honour Bowling of this Parish and Joseph Dunman of Washington Parish,
   Jan. 4, 1726/7.
B. Margaret, dau. of William and Eleanor Bowling, Aug. 15, 1727.
M. Simon Bowling and Elizabeth Newport, June 5, 1728.
M. Bethridge Bowling and Daniel Hammit, Nov. 2, 1728.
M. Thomas Bowling and Rachel Colclough, Nov. 11, 1729.
B. Anne, dau. of Simon and Martha Bowling, Feb. 20, 1730/1.
D. Robert Bowling, Mar. 17, 1730/1.
B. Anne, dau. of William and Sarah Bowling, June 9, 1731.
B. John Kidwell, son of William and Elizabeth Bowling, Sept. 13, 1731.
M. Samuel Bowling and Elizabeth Oxford, Oct. 8, 1731.
B. Priscilla, dau. of Thomas and Rachel Bowling, Mar. 7, 1731/2.
B. Benjamin, son of Benjamin and Mary Bowling, Sept. 18, 1732.
B. William, son of William and Sarah Bowling, May 13, 1733.
B. Sophia, dau. of Simon and Martha Bowling, Oct. 8, 1733.
B. Mary, dau. of Samuel and Mary Bowling, Nov. 4, 1734.
B. John, son of Benjamin and Mary Bowling, Nov. 10, 1734.
B. Elizabeth, dau. of William and Sarah Bowling, June 10, 1735.
D. Simon Bowling, Oct. 25, 1735.
B. Robert, son of Simon Bowling, dec'd., and Martha his wife, Oct. 26, 1735.
D. Martha Bowling, Oct. 29, 1735.
B. Eleanor, dau. of Samuel and Elizabeth Bowling, Nov. 30, 1735.
D. Mary Bowling, Dec. 5, 1735.
B. Honor, dau. of William and Sarah Bowling, Mar. 8, 1736/7.
M. Mary Bowling and William Eaton, Aug. 25, 1737.

B. Elizabeth, dau. of Samuel and Elizabeth Bowling, Oct. 28, 1737.
B. Stephen, son of Thomas and Rachel Bowling, Jan. 26, 1738/9.
M. Joseph Bowling and Pelatiah Crafford, July 15, 1738.
B. Samuel, son of Samuel and Elizabeth Bowling, Feb. 9, 1739/40.
B. Mary, dau. of William and Sarah Bowling, July 7, 1740.
B. William, son of Samuel and Elizabeth Bowling, Apr. 20, 1741.
M. David Bowling and Jane Pilcher, Sept. 10, 1741.
B. Sarah, dau. of William and Sarah Bowling, May 30, 1742.
B. Jesse, son of David and Jane Bowling, June 1, 1742.
B. Margaret, dau. of Samuel and Elizabeth Bowling, Mar. 26, 1743.
B. Benjamin, son of Samuel and Elizabeth Bowling, Aug. 15, 1744.
B. Anne, dau. of Samuel and Elizabeth Bowling, Feb. 11, 1745/6.
B. James, son of Elizabeth Booing (Bowling?), Sept. 8, 1746.
B. James, son of Samuel and Elizabeth Bowling, Feb. 20, 1747/8.
M. Behethland Bowling and John Day, Feb. 21, 1747/8.
M. James Bowling and Mary Overall, Feb. 11, 1750/1.
M. Rachel Bowling and Joseph Doody (Moody?), Feb. 13, 1750/1.
M. Original Bowling and Margaret French, Mar. 18, 1752.
B. William, son of Rachel Bowling, Nov. 25, 1754.
D. Captain Samuel Bowman, July 14, 1742.
M. George Boyle and Mary Whiting, June 2, 1778.
B. Elizabeth, dau. of Thomas and Sarah Bradley, May 26, 1732.
M. Mary Anne Bradshaw and James P. Bowie, Sept. 16, 1788.
M. Uriah Bradshaw and Keziah Bragg, Feb. 23, 1791.
M. Margaret Brady and Richard Lee, July 8, 1723.
M. Keziah Bragg and Uriah Bradshaw, Feb. 23, 1791.
D. Amy Brandegan, June 23, 1741.
M. Susanna Brandison and Samuel Wells, July 8, 1723.
M. Thomas Bradley and Sarah Carver, Jan. 8, 1731/2.
B. Elizabeth, dau. of John and Mary Branham, Feb. 15, 1735/6.
B. Mary, dau. of John and Mary Branham, Feb. 5, 1738/9.
D. John Branham, Sept. 27, 1742.
B. Chloe, dau. of John and Mary Branham, Mar. 8, 1742/3.
M. Mary Branham and John Davis, Sept. 8, 1745.
M. Mary Branner and Anderson White, Oct. 14, 1794.
D. John Branson, Oct. 24, 1716.
M. Josiah Bransam and Barbara Lindsay, Oct. 5, 1742.
M. Katherine Branson and Moses Grigsby of Overwharton Parish, Dec. 1, 1742.
M. Zachariah Brazier and Elizabeth Buckner, Nov. 12, 1759.
B. William, son of William and Jane Brent of Richland, July 26, 1733.
B. Giles, son of William and Jane Brent of Richland, Sept. 17, 1735.
B. Henry, son of William and Sarah Briant, Apr. 9, 1756.
B. William, son of William and Mary Briant, Mar. 9, 1760.
M. William Briant and Elizabeth Simpson, June 21, 1779.
M. William Briant and Ursula Burridge, Feb. 27, 1782.
M. Jesse Briant and Anne Norman, Jan. 1, 1790.
M. Mary Bridges of Overwharton Parish and John Devean, Aug. 4, 1764.
M. David Briggs and Jane McDonald, June 1, 1771.
B. Patrick, son of Patrick and Catherine Brinton (Bruiston?) June 2, 1757.
M. Elizabeth Briscoe and Andrew Drummond, Jan. 16, 1735/6.
M. Anne Brisse and James Baxter, June 7, 1767.
M. Sarah Broadburn and Thomas Bunbury, Oct. 15, 1723.
M. Jane Brockenburg and Thomas Pratt, June 23, 1785.
M. John Brooke and Lucy Thornton, July 2, 1777.
M. Mary Brooke and Elias Rose, Mar. 30, 1778.
B. John, son of Mary Brookes, Mar. 19, 1773.

M. James Brown and Isabel Ross, June 4, 1726.
M. Charity Brown and Isaac Settle, Sept. 24, 1726.
B. Joyce, dau. of Daniel and Elizabeth Brown, Mar. 12, 1727/8.
B. George, son of Daniel Brown, Dec. 23, 1742.
M. William Brown and Elizabeth Butler, Aug. 2, 1744.
B. John, son of William and Elizabeth Brown, Feb. 18, 1744/5.
B. Butler, son of William and Elizabeth Brown, Apr. 10, 1747.
B. William, son of William and Elizabeth Brown, Sept. 23, 1748.
B. Mildred, dau. of William and Elizabeth Brown, Dec. 26, 1757.
M. James Brown and Sarah Waemark, May 11, 1760.
B. James, son of William and Elizabeth Brown, Aug. 1, 1761.
B. James (?), son of Samuel and Jane Brown, Nov. 30, 1771.
M. Thomas Brown and Mildred Smith, Dec. 16, 1773.
M. Parthenia Brown and Samuel Franks, Jan. 19, 1786.
M. James Brown and Hannah Mills, Jan. 31, 1786.
M. William Bruce and Lucinda Pollard, Dec. 20, 1787.
M. William Bruton and Elizabeth Spicer (Spiller?), June 5, 1725 (1724)
B. Mary, dau. of William and Elizabeth Bruton, July 4, 1725.
D. Elizabeth Bruton, a child, May 31, 1728.
B. Elizabeth, dau. of William and Elizabeth Bruerton (sic) Jan. 25, 1726/7.
D. Thomas, son of William and Elizabeth Bruton, Oct. 3, 1728.
B. Elizabeth, dau. of William and Elinor Bruton, Jan. 15, 1727/8.
B. John, son of William and Mary Bryan, May 24, 1735.
B. William, son of William and Mary Bryan, May 6, 1739.
D. Nathaniel Bryant, Mar. 23, 1732/3.
M. John Bryant and Sarah Graham, Dec. 11, 1768.
M. Monica Bryant and John Addison, Mar. 19, 1789.
M. James Buchanan and Elizabeth Limmit, Dec. 7, 1777.
B. Henry, son of Henry and Tabitha Buckeridge, June 12, 1768.
M. Dorothy Buckley and Thomas South, July 10, 1754.
D. Robert Buckner, Oct. 25, 1718.
D. Elizabeth Buckner, Nov. 14, 1725.
D. William Buckner, Nov. 11, 1725.
D. William Buckner, Aug. 3, 1727.
D. Anthony Buckner, Mar. 21, 1733/4.
D. Anthony Buckner, Dec. 1, 1734.
M. Sarah Buckner and Thomas Price, Dec. 31, 1734.
D. Major John Buckner, May 6, 1748.
B. Susan, dau. of John and Elizabeth Buckner, Sept. 1, 1751.
B. Parthenia, dau. of Anthony and Amy Buckner, Oct. 14, 1758.
M. Elizabeth Buckner and Zachariah Brazier, Nov. 12, 1759.[9]
M. John Buckner and Elizabeth Washington, Dec. 21, 1760.
M. Thomas Bunbury and Sarah Broadburn, Oct. 15, 1723.
D. William Bunbury, Nov. 16, 1725.
B. John, son of Thomas and Sarah Bunbury, Jan. 2, 1725/6.
M. Dulcibella Bunbury and Enoch Berry, Dec. 12, 1726.
B. William, son of Thomas and Sarah Bunbury, Jan. 26, 1726/7.
B. Mildred, dau. of Thomas and Sarah Bunbury, Sept. 2, 1731.
B. Dulcibella, dau. of Thomas and Sarah Bunbury, Sept. 15, 1733.
B. Elizabeth, dau. of Thomas and Sarah Bunbury, Apr. 25, 1736.
D. Frances Bunbury, Apr. 4, 1737.
B. Frances, dau. of Thomas and Sarah Bunbury, Sept. 1, 1738.
M. Jane Bunbury and George Hardin, Dec. 3, 1740.
B. Anne and Jane, daus. of Thos. and Sarah Bunbury, Nov. 12, 1741.
M. Katherine Bunbury and Cossum Bennett, Jan. 7, 1742/3.
B. Sarah, dau. of Thomas and Sarah Bunbury, Mar. 9, 1743/4.

M. Dulcibella Bunbury and Withers Conway, Apr. 21, 1752.
M. Thomas Bunbury and Behethland Massey, Aug. 30, 1752.
B. Elizabeth, dau. of Thomas and Behethland Bunbury, Jan. 30, 1756.
M. Mildred Bunbury and William Scott, June 18, 1756.
M. Frances Bunbury and Alexander Scott, Feb. 22, 1758.
M. Anne Bunbury and Richard Fowke, Mar. 16, 1760.
B. Anne dau. of Thomas and Behethland Bunbury, July 1, 1764.
M. Jane Bunbury and Joseph Sanford, May 8, 1766.
M. Elizabeth Bunbury and Stephen Chandler, Dec. 24, 1774.
M. Frances Bunbury and William Smoot, Sept. 23, 1775.
M. William Bunbury and Elizabeth Short, Jan. 16, 1783.
B. Mary, dau. of Richard and Mary Burgess, Nov. 3, 1736.
M. Lettice Burgess and John Engles, Feb. 15, 1736/7.
B. Edward, son of Edward and Margaret Burgess, Nov. 27, 1739.
B. Moses, son of Edward and Margaret Burgess, Dec. 2, 1742.
B. Reuben, son of Edward and Margaret Burgess, Feb. 12, 1744/5.
M. Joseph Burgess and Elizabeth Douglas, July 15, 1749.
M. Anne Burgess and Joseph Rogers, Oct. 24, 1749.
M. Margaret Burgess and John French, Jan. 15, 1749/50.
M. Mary Burgess and Nathan Skipwith White, Apr. 15, 1759.
M. Moses Burgess and Elizabeth Price, May 30, 1762.
B. Lunsford, son of Moses and Elizabeth Burgess, Sept. 20, 1762.
B. John Buckner, son of Moses Burgess, Apr. 5, 1764.
M. Edward Burgess and Mary (?) Price, Feb. 20, 1765.
M. Reuben Burgess and Margaret Stribling, Sept. 1, 1765.
B. Edward, son of Moses and Elizabeth Burgess, Apr. 2, 1767.
B. Mary, dau. of Reuben and Margaret Burgess, July 11, 1767.
B. William, son of Reuben and Margaret Burgess, June 15, 1769.
B. Reuben, son of Reuben and Margaret Burgess, June 14, 1772.
B. William, son of Thomas and Jane Burke, Apr. 2, 1752.
M. William Burke and Susanna Sweeny, Feb. 1, 1778.
M. John Burkett and Mary Carnady, Sept. 27, 1735.
D. John Burkett, Oct. 1, 1736.
B. Eleanor, dau. of John and Mary Burkett, Jan. 2, 1736/7.
M. Mary Burkett and Thomas Norfolk, Dec. 6, 1737.
M. John Burkett and Elizabeth Skidmore, Aug. 6, 1751.
B. James, son of Elizabeth Burkesworth, Feb. 22, 1730/1.
M. Thomas Burnett and Alice Cave of Hanover Parish, June 20, 1746.
B. Mary, dau. of Joseph and Eleanor Burnoim, Feb. 28, 1772.
M. Jethro Burnsplat and Sarah Bagjob, Oct. 21, 1729.
B. Sarah, dau. of Jethro and Sarah Burnsplat, Jan. 16, 1731/2.
B. Eleanor, dau. of Jethro and Sarah Burnsplat, Mar. 2, 1735/6.
D. Jethro Burnsplat, Nov. 2, 1737.
M. Sarah Burnsplat and Richard Hill, Dec. 22, 1737.
M. Eleanor Burnsplat and James Kelly, Apr. 15, 1757.
M. Ursula Burridge and William Briant, Feb. 27, 1782.
M. William Burton and Sarah Spicer, Dec. 14, 1725.
B. Lettice, dau. of William and Sarah Burton, Aug. 19, 1726.[10]
B. Mary, dau. of William and Rachel Burton, May 30, 1754.[10]
M. Charity Bush and Peter Cash, Nov. 3, 1729.
M. George Bush and Mary Ancrum, Nov. 14, 1737.
B. William, son of George and Mary Bush, Sept. 8, 1738. [11]
B. Frances, dau. of George and Mary Bush, Apr. 20, 1741.[11]
M. Frances Bush and Joshua Skidmore, Aug. 6, 1751.
M. John Bushell and Elizabeth Mason, June 26, 1748.
M. John Bushell and Molly Dodd, Dec. 18, 1791.

B. George, son of Elizabeth Bussee, May 20, 1731.
M. Sarah Bussey and Ralph Walker, Jan. 26, 1722/3.
D. Martha Bussey, June 23, 1725.
B. Sarah, dau. of Henry and Elizabeth Bussey, Jan. 22, 1730/1.
B. Anne, dau. of Henry and Elizabeth Bussey, Apr. 19, 1734.
D. Elizabeth Bussey, July 20, 1739.
M. Henry Bussey and Margaret McCarty, July 11, 1741.
B. Henry, son of Henry and Margaret Bussey, Apr. 13, 1743.
B. Cornelius, son of Henry and Margaret Bussey, June 18, 1745.
M. Anne Bussey and John Matthews, July 21, 1754.
M. Mary Bussey and Thomas Mills, Jan. 2, 1748/9.
M. Henry Bussey and Jane Jackson, Nov. 21, 1758.
M. Jane Bussey and William Bentley, Mar. 14, 1765.
M. Cornelius Bussey and Mary Carver, Oct. 14, 1770.
M. Cornelius Bussey and Jane Crawford, June 23, 1776.
Bapt. John, son of Thomas and Elizabeth Butler, Mar. 6, 1719/20.
B. Mary and Elizabeth, daus. of Thomas and Elizabeth Butler, Feb. 15, 1724/5.
D. Mary and Elizabeth, daus. of Thomas and Elizabeth Butler, Feb. 18, 1724/5.
D. Elizabeth, wife of Thomas Butler, Sept. 22, 1727.
B. Elizabeth, dau. of Thomas and Elizabeth Butler, Apr. 15, 1726.
D. Thomas Butler, July 10, 1728.
M. Sarah Butler of this Parish and Charles Ashton of Washington Parish, Sept. 22, 1733.
M. John Butler and Elizabeth Clement, Feb. 19, 1733/4.
M. Jane Butler and William Knight, Dec. 26, 1734.
D. Elizabeth Butler, Jan. 19, 1736/7.
B. Katherine, dau. of James and Sarah Butler, Aug. 24, 1737.
B. Margaret, dau. of James and Sarah Butler, Dec. 27, 1739.
M. Jane Butler and George Blankenship, Feb. 12, 1739/40.
B. John, son of James and Sarah Butler, Dec. 27, 1740.
M. Thomas Butler of Washington Parish and Anne Baxter, Sept. 22, 1742.
B. Sarah, dau. of James and Sarah Butler, Jan. 17, 1742/3.
M. Elizabeth Butler and William Brown, Aug. 2, 1744.
B. Thomas, son of James and Sarah Butler, Aug. 30, 1747.
B. Joseph, son of Henry and Anne Buttrage, July 29, 1759.
B. Violetta, dau. of John and Elizabeth Buttridge, Sept. 4, 1764.
M. Henry Buttridge and Isabel Hodge, Dec. 30, 1764.
B. William Matthews, son of John and Elizabeth Buttridge, July 3, 1767.
M. Violetta Buttridge and James Cockley, Jan. 12, 1786.
B. Anne, dau. of James and Bridget Buzell, Aug. 21, 1738.
B. George, son of Thomas and Jane Byrne, Mar. 16, 1760.

C

M. David Cable and Mary Orr, Sept. 7, 1766.
M. Elizabeth Calb and William Clift, Jan. 16, 1764.
D. John Calico, Sept. 19, 1717.
B. John, son of John Calico, dec'd., and Rebecca, Feb. 19, 1717/18.
D. John, son of John and Rebecca Calico, May 12, 1720.
M. Frances Call and Thomas Sweatman, Dec. 16, 1765.
D. James (?) Campbell, Nov. 27, 1725.
M. Mary Campbell and Edward Dulaney, Apr. 15, 1726.
M. Katherine Campbell and John Raymond, Jan. 12, 1735/6.
M. John Campbell and Judith Pilcher of Hanover Parish, Aug. 20, 1746.
B. William, son of Katherine Campbell, June 12, 1747.
B. James, son of Christian Campbell, July 17, 1747.

M. Katherine Campbell and Francis Allen, Nov. 17, 1747.
M. Archibald Campbell and Rebecca Rawlings, Jan. 15, 1753.
M. Alexander Campbell and Lucy Fitzhugh, Dec. 3, 1788.
M. Margaret Cannady and Benjamin Derrick, Aug. 3, 1734.
M. Anne Caplee and John Tracy of Washington Parish, Aug. 7, 1740.
M. Mary Carnady and John Burkett, Sept. 27, 1735.
M. Hugh Carnady and Mildred Hutcheson, Nov. 6, 1735.
M. Sarah Carrico and Joseph King, May 7, 1731.
M. Thomas Carrico and Jane McCant, Oct. 4, 1744.
B. John, son of Thomas and Jane Carrico, Oct. 7, 1745.
B. Alexander, son of Thomas and Sarah Carrico, Feb. 10, 1746/7.
D. Thomas Carrico, Feb. 5, 1748/9.
M. Rosamond Carroll of Brunswich Parish and Joseph Tucker, Feb. 20, 1733/4.
M. Mary Carroll and George Harrison, July 14, 1750.
B. Elizabeth Leftwich, dau. of John and Sarah Carroll, Mar. 8, 1753.
M. Martha Carruthers of Overwharton Parish and James McDonald, Nov. 15, 1732.
M. Helena Carter and Richard Turner, Sept. 24, 1725.
M. Anne Carter and John Champe, jun: Apr. 17, 1762.
B. Anne, dau. of Richard & Anne Carver, Mar. 1, 1715/6.
M. Richard Carver and Sarah Jones, Jan. 21, 1722/3.
B. John, son of Richard and Sarah Carver, Mar. 19, 1726/7.
M. Thomas Carver and Mary Clift, Nov. 10, 1727.
D. Joseph Carver, Dec. 20, 1727.
M. Sarah Carver and Thomas Bradley, Jan. 8, 1731/2.
B. Joseph, son of Thomas and Mary Carver, Nov. 11, 1732.
D. Richard Carver, Dec. 6, 1732.
M. Frances Carver and John Sudduth, June 8, 1733.
B. Jane, dau. of Richard and Sarah Carver, June 23, 1733.
B. Thomas, son of Thomas and Mary Carver, Feb. 20, 1734/5.
B. William, son of Thomas and Mary Carver, July 5, 1737.
M. John Carver and Elizabeth Doggett, Aug. 31, 1757.
B. William, son of Sarah Carver, Nov. 15, 1737.
B. Sarah, dau. of Thomas and Mary Carver, Sept. 13, 1739.
B. Charles, son of Mary Carver, July 28, 1741.
B. Joseph, son of Thomas and Mary Carver, Feb. 17, 1742/3.
B. Jane, dau. of Thomas and Mary Carver, July 1, 1745.
B. Jane, dau. of Thomas and Mary Carver, Jan. 10, 1747/8.
M. Anne Carver and Burgess Sullivan, Feb. 3, 1747/8.
B. Polly, dau. of Thomas and Mary Carver, Oct. 13, 1750.
B. Frances, dau. of Thomas and Mary Carver, Jan. 24, 1754.
M. Thomas Carver and Rosamond Duncomb, Aug. 12, 1755.
B. Thomas, son of William and Sarah Carver, Nov. 2, 1757.
B. Betty, dau. of John and Hannah Carver, Feb. 2, 1760.
B. Molly, dau. of John and Susan Carver, Mar. 26, 1762.
B. Mildred, dau. of William and Mary Carver, May 10, 1762.
B. William, son of William and Sarah Carver, Jan. 4, 1764.
M. Sarah Carver and Daniel Taylour, Jan. 19, 1764.
B. Jane, dau. of Joseph and Elizabeth Carver, Dec. 25, 1765.
M. Jane Carver and Dennis Mehorner, Sept. 8, 1766.
B. William, son of Joseph and Elizabeth Carver, Jan. 9, 1767.
B. Reuben, son of Charles and Mary Carver, Oct. 10, 1767.
M. John Carver and Mary Rose, July 17, 1768.
B. Frances, dau. of Joseph and Elizabeth Carver, Jan. 12, 1769.
B. Elizabeth, dau. of Joseph and Elizabeth Carver, Aug. 12, 1770.
M. Mary Carver and Cornelius Bussey, Oct. 14, 1770.
B. John, son of Charles and Anne Carver, Jan. 27, 1771.

B. Susanna, dau. of Robert and Jane Carver, Apr. 18, 1771.
B. Reuben, son of Joseph and Elizabeth Carver, Apr. 12, 1772.
B. Anne, dau. of John and Mary Carver, May 19, 1773.
B. Joseph, son of Joseph and Elizabeth Carver, Jan. 24, 1775.
B. Thomas, son of Joseph and Elizabeth Carver, May 10, 1774.
B. Reuben, son of Joseph and Elizabeth Carver, Nov. 1, 1777.
B. Henry, son of Joseph and Elizabeth Carver, Nov. 30, 1779.
M. Molly Carver and William Whitmore, Jan. 5, 1781.
B. George, son of Joseph and Elizabeth Carver, Sept. 10, 1782.
M. John Carver and Hannah Clift, Apr. 14, 1784.
M. Dully Carver and Charles Philips, Aug. 19, 1787.
B. Moses, son of William and Anne Cash, Mar. 9, 1717/18.
D. William Cash, Apr. 2, 1720.
D. John Cash, Sept. 25, 1729.
M. Peter Cash and Charity Bush, Nov. 3, 1729.
B. Jane, dau. of Peter and Charity Cash, Mar. 6, 1732/3.
B. John, son of Peter and Charity Cash, Sept. 3, 1735.
B. Frances, dau. of Peter and Charity Cash, Nov. 9, 1738.
B. Katherine, dau. of Peter and Charity Cash, Mar. 9, 1740/1.
B. Charity, dau. of Peter and Charity Cash, Nov. 26, 1743.[12]
M. Stephen Cash and Jemima Grining, May 26, 1747.
M. Margaret Cash and Josias Stone, Apr. 8, 1780.
M. George Catlett and Mary Harrison, Nov. 23, 1758.
M. Alice Cave of Hanover Parish and Thomas Burnett, June 20, 1746.
M. Rose Cavenaugh and Matthew Jones, Sept. 21, 1746.
M. Anne Chambers and Jasper Lloyd, Jan. 7, 1717/18.
M. Anne Chambers and William Garrett, Jan. 28, 1717/8.
M. Elinor Chambers and Patrick Johnson, May 14, 1726.
M. John Champe, jun: and Anne Carter, Apr. 17, 1762.
M. Thomas Chancellor and Katherine Cooper, Mar. 3, 1723/4.
M. John Chandler and Behethland Rogers, Sept. 17, 1767.
B. Stephen, son of John and Behethland Chandler, July 6, 1768.
B. William Rogers, son of John and Behethland Chandler, Sept. 27, 1772.
M. Stephen Chandler and Elizabeth Bunbury, Dec. 24, 1774.
M. Pearson Chapman and Susanna Alexander, July 31, 1766.
B. Nathaniel, son of Pearson and Susanna Chapman, June 27, 1767.
B. Anne, dau. of Cornelius and Virgin Cheesman, Feb. 22, 1717/8.
D. Virgin Cheesman, Mar. 8, 1720/1.
M. Grace Cheesman and Richard Vincent, Dec. 31, 1730.
B. Jacob, son of Anne Cheesman, Aug. 10, 1734.
M. Anne Cheesman and George Johnson, Jan. 9, 1734/5.
D. Cornelius Cheesman, Feb. 9, 1747/8.
M. Kenelm Cheseldine and Frances Taliaferro, Aug. 9, 1768.
M. Richard Chidley and Sarah Fox, Dec. 21, 1722.
B. Rawleigh, son of Rawleigh and Sarah Chinn, Jan. 22, 1758.[13]
B. William, son of John and Margaret Christie, May 27, 1720.
M. Margaret Christie and Henry Smith, May 28, 1723.
M. John Christie and Sarah Glover, Aug. 28, 1743.
B. William, son of John and Mary Christie, Nov. 15, 1745.
B. John, son of John and Sarah Christie, Jan. 10, 1747/8.
D. Sarah, wife of John Christie, Dec. 6, 1748.
M. John Christie and Mary Ryan, May 4, 1749.
B. Anne, dau. of John and Mary Christie, Feb. 16, 1750/1.
M. John Christie and Elizabeth Griggs, Sept. 12, 1751.
M. Charles Christie and Anne Smith, Mar. 18, 1753.
B. Charity, dau. of John and Elizabeth Christie, Aug. 21, 1754.

B. Peggy, dau. of John and Elizabeth Christie, Feb. 17, 1757.
B. James, son of John and Elizabeth Christie, Jan. 24, 1761.
M. John Christie and Frances Johnson, Jan. 20, 1771.
M. William Christie and Margaret Thompson, June 6, 1775.
M. John Christie and Elizabeth Gray Dudley, Oct. 7, 1785.
M. John Clanton of Hanover parish and Anne Spicer of this Parish, Feb. 17, 1731/2.
B. Benjamin, son of John and Anne Clanton, Nov. 20, 1732.
M. Elizabeth Clark and John Diskins, Apr. 21, 1724.
M. William Clark of Overwharton Parish and Sarah Sanders of St. Paul's, Aug. 5, 1752.
B. William, son of Moses Clark, Dec. 29, 1757.
B. George, son of Moses and Susan Clark, Jan. 26, 1760.
M. Patrick Clark and Tabitha Kelly, Aug. 13, 1764.
M. Mary Clark and David Nevins, June 28, 1767.
M. Charles Clark and Phoebe Derrick, Dec. 14, 1785.
M. Mary Clark and James Tolmark, May 17, 1792.
D. Grace Clement, Aug. 6, 1727.
M. Edward Clement and Elizabeth Fawyn, Oct. 25, 1728.
D. Edward Clement, June 20, 1733.
M. Elizabeth Clement and John Butler, Feb. 19, 1733/4.
B. Benjamin and Sarah, son and dau. of John and Hannah Clift, Aug. 5, 1717.
D. Hannah Clift, Nov. 27, 1725.
M. Mary Clift and Thomas Carver, Nov. 10, 1727.
M. William Clift and Mary Hill, Jan. 19, 1730/1.
M. John Clift and Margaret Johns, Mar. 2, 1738/9.
M. Sarah Clift and John Lindsay, Jan. 3, 1739/40.
B. William, son of John and Mary Clift, Mar. 28, 1740.
M. Benjamin Clift and Margaret Sebastian, May 6, 1740.
B. John, son of John and Margaret Clift, May 13, 1742.
B. William, son of John and Margaret Clift, Oct. 28, 1742.
M. Joseph Clift and Joyce Barrett, June 22, 1743.
B. Thomas, son of Joseph and Joyce Clift, Sept. 22, 1744.
M. John Clift and Mary Beach, July 2, 1745.
B. Nanny, dau. of Benjamin and Margaret Clift, May 6, 1746.
B. Robert, son of John and Mary Clift, Sept. 6, 1746.
B. Hannah, dau. of Joseph and Joyce Clift, May 5, 1748.
B. Benjamin, son of John and Mary Clift, Jan. 17, 1748/9.
B. Joseph, son of Robert and Jane Clift, Dec. 5, 1750.
B. Henry, son of John and Mary Clift, Jan. 4, 1750/1.
B. Catherine, dau. of Robert and Jane Clift, Feb. 26, 1753.
B. Polly, dau. of John and Mary Clift, Sept. 28, 1753.
B. Billy, son of Benjamin and Margaret Clift, Jan. 22, 1754.
B. Anne, dau. of Robert and Jane Clift, Aug. 6, 1755.
B. Sarah, dau. of John Clift, Nov. 5, 1756.
B. Jane, dau. of Robert and Jane Clift, Feb. 3, 1758.
B. Hannah, dau. of John and Mary Clift, Feb. 26, 1760.
B. Molly, dau. of Robert and Jane Clift, May 23, 1760.
B. Robert, son of Robert and Jane Clift, Sept. 21, 1762.
M. William Clift and Elizabeth Calb, Jan. 16, 1764.
B. Reuben, son of John and Mary Clift, July 6, 1764.
B. John, son of Robert and Jane Clift, Nov. 12, 1764.
M. Benjamin Clift and Frances Peake, Feb. 16, 1772.
M. Benjamin Clift and Sarah Rogers, Dec. 6, 1772.
M. Robert Clift and Elizabeth Bolling, Jan. 21, 1777.
M. John Clift and Jemima Arnold, Dec. 26, 1777.
M. John Clift and Anne Rogers, Sept. 29, 1779.

M. Caty Clift and Hosea Rogers, Jan. 22, 1783.
M. Hannah Clift and John Carver, Apr. 14, 1784.
M. Dully Clift and John Scott, Feb. 15, 1787.
M. Robert Clift and Peggy Munday, Jan. 6, 1793.
M. Anne Clifton and William Scott, Feb. 23, 1727/8.
M. Burdet Clifton and Frances Hill, July 15, 1733.
B. Thomas, son of Burdet and Frances Clifton, Apr. 20, 1734.
B. Burdet and Baldwin, sons of Burdet and Frances Clifton, Feb. 3, 1735/6.
B. Anne, dau. of Burdet and Frances Clifton, Aug. 24, 1737.
B. Sarah, dau. of Burdet and Frances Clifton, Apr. 10, 1740.
B. Jane and Elizabeth, daus. of Burdet and Frances Clifton, May 14, 1743.
M. Burdet Clifton and Grace Seaton, May 18, 1745.
B. Henry, son of Burdet and Grace Clifton, Mar. 17, 1745/6.
B. Charles, son of Burdet and Grace Clifton, Dec. 12, 1747.
B. John, son of Thomas and Anne Clifton, Feb. 7, 1758.
M. Anne Clifton and Price Stuart, Oct. 17, 1781.
M. John (?) Coad and Elizabeth Massey, Dec. 6, 1766.
M. James Cockley and Violetta Buttridge, Jan. 12, 1786.
D. (John) Coggins, Apr. 29, 1717.
M. Rose Coggins and William Cooke, July 22, 1717.
M. John Coggins and Sophia Gotbey, Feb. 22, 1736/7.
B. Anna, dau. of John and Sophia Coggins, Mar. 30, 1737.
B. Amos, son of John and Sophia Coggins, Mar. 23, 1738/9.
B. Betty, dau. of John and Sophia Coggins, Nov. 13, 1740.
B. William and Alexander, sons of Benjamin and Rachel Colclough, July 2, 1717.
B. Sarah, dau. of Benjamin and Rachel Colclough, Mar. 17, 1719/20.
M. Hester Colclough and Joel Stripling, Sept. 25, 1723.
M. Rachel Colclough and Thomas Bowling, Nov. 11, 1729.
D. Alexander Colclough, Nov. 10, 1739.
M. Jane Colclough and Benjamin Newton of Hamilton Parish, Oct. 22, 1740.
M. William Colclough and Mary Roger, Dec. 30, 1741.
B. John, son of William and Mary Colclough, Sept. 14, 1743.
B. Margaret, dau. of William and Mary Colclough, Feb. 4, 1744/5.
B. Elizabeth, dau. of William and Mary Colclough, Oct. 11, 1747.
D. Rachel Colclough, Dec. 25, 1748.
B. Samuel Cole a Musteo (?) May 6, 1726.
B. James, son of Anne Coleworth, Sept. 30, 1747.
B. Elizabeth, dau. of Mary Collins, Nov. 25, 1736.
M. Mary Collins and William Stevenson, Sept. 24, 1761.
B. Mary, dau. of John and Elizabeth Collins, Mar. 22, 1762.
M. Margaret Colvin and William Ancrum, Dec. 24, 1734.
B. Mason, son of Daniel Colvin, Feb. 26, 1764 (Overwharton).
M. John Conoli and Helen Foy, June 22, 1724.
M. John Conali and Elinor Ormand, June 13, 1725.
D. Elinor Connor, a servant woman of Samuel Todd, Sept. 3, 1718.
B. Withers, son of Christopher and Sarah Conway, Aug. 20, 1717.
M. Elizabeth Conway and John Alsop, Dec. 30, 1739.
M. Withers Conway and Dulcibella Bunbury, Apr. 21, 1752.
B. Miles Withers, son of Withers and Dulcibella Conway, Mar. 2, 1753.
B. John Withers, son of Withers and Dulcibella Conway, Sept. 12, 1757.
B. Anne, dau. of Withers and Dulcibella Conway, Apr. 13, 1764.
M. William Cooke and Rose Coggins, July 22, 1717.
M. Rose Cooke and William Hawkins, Aug. 16, 1723.
M. Joseph Cooke and Mary Trenar, Dec. 26, 1723.
B. Elizabeth, dau. of William and Elizabeth Cooper, May 5, 1718.

M. Elizabeth Cooper and Jasper Floyd, Dec. 4, 1723.
M. Katherine Cooper and Thomas Chancellor, Mar. 3, 1723/4.
B. John, son of William and Elizabeth (?Cooper), -- 1729.
B. Jane, dau. of Mary Cooper, Dec. 5, 1737.
B. James, son of Elizabeth Cooper, Dec. 8, 1740.
M. Elizabeth Cooper and Robert Sudduth, Oct. 2, 1750.
M. James Cope and Elizabeth Mifflin of Hanover Parish, Dec. 17, 1746.
M. Katherine Copley and John Wilkinson, Aug. 14, 1743.
M. Margaret Corbin and William Griffin, Apr. 6, 1725.
M. John Corbin and Lettice Lee, Sept. 1, 1737.
M. Rosamond Corbin of this Parish and John Spinks of Brunswick Parish, Nov. 6, 1741.
M. Mary Cotes and Samuel Wilkinson, Dec. 9, 1734.
M. James Couch (?Gouch) and Elizabeth Powers of Caroline, Feb. 21, 1762.
M. Anne Coventry and Joseph Sebastian, Sept. 8, 1751.
B. Matthew Cox, son of Matthew and Mary Cox, Sept. 19, 1745.
M. Richard Cox and Anne Crismund, Sept. 2, 1750.
B. Pelatiah, dau. of Philip and Pelatiah Crafford, June 4, 1718.
B. Philip, son of Philip and Pelatiah Crafford, 1723.
D. Pelatiah Crafford, June 18, 1725.
M. Philip Crafford and Mary Simmons, Nov. 27, 1730.
B. Peter, son of Philip and Mary Crafford, Sept. 15, 1731.
B. William, son of Philip and Mary Crafford, Nov. 2, 1734.
D. John Crafford, Dec. 20, 1736 (?1733).
M. Pelatiah Crafford and Joseph Bowling, July 15, 1738.
B. Mary, dau. of Mary Crafford, Mar. 4, 1738/9.
M. Peter Crafford and Jane Gladsteans, Aug. 7, 1755.[14]
M. Jane Crafford (?Crawford) and Cornelius Bussye, June 23, 1776.
M. William Crank and Sabra Jones, Feb. 8, 1778.
D. Mary Crannidge, Sept. 30, 1716.
B. Honor, dau. of Jeremy and Anne Crannidge, Feb. 2, 1717/8.
D. Honor Crannidge, June 26, 1735.
M. Samuel Crannidge and Elizabeth Day, May 6, 1741.
B. Mary, dau. of Samuel and Elizabeth Crannidge, Sept. 20, 1741.
B. Jane, dau. of Samuel and Elizabeth Crannidge, Oct. 8, 1743.
B. Samuel, son of Samuel and Elizabeth Crannidge, Mar. 12, 1744/5.
M. Anne Crismund and Richard Cox, Sept. 2, 1750.
M. Joseph Crismund and Elizabeth Purtle, Feb. 16, 1752.
M. Oswald Crismund and Jane Rose, June 27, 1757.
B. Oswald, son of Oswald and Jane Crismund, Sept. 2, 1760.
B. Charles, son of Oswald and Jane Crismund, Aug. 8, 1764.
B. John, son of Oswald and Jane Crismund, Mar. 27, 1766.
M. William Crismund and Anne Tregar, Apr. 28, 1779.
M. Robert Crook and Mary Gosling, Apr. 15, 1745.[15]
BAPT: John, son of Dennis and Margaret Crugers, June 6, 1725.
B. Thomas, son of Adam and Anna Barbara Crump, Feb. 17, 1734/5.
B. John, son of Adam and Anna Barbara Crump, Sept. 28, 1736.
D. Anna Barbara Crump, Dec. 12, 1737.
M. William Crysell and Frances Rose, Nov. 17, 1782.
M. John Culham and Lettice Sudduth, Feb. 17, 1775.
M. James Cullings and Sarah Hutton, Feb. 14, 1755.
M. Peter Culvey and Sarah Sweeny, Mar. 28, 1758.
M. Morris Cunningham and Anne Poplar, Apr. 2, 1738.
B. Phoebe, dau. of Morris and Anne Cunningham, Apr. 6, 1739.
M. James Cunningham and Behethland Overall, June 21, 1757.
M. John Curley and Mary Maddox, May 9, 1767.

B. David, son of John and Mary Curley, Feb. 16, 1773.
M. John Curry and Jane Stribling, Sept. 20, 1758.
M. Jane Curry and William Peck, Aug. 3, 1766.
M. John Curry and Anne Rogers, Dec. 25, 1783.

D

B. Baldwin, son of Townshend and Elizabeth Dade, Oct. 13, 1716.
D. Jane, dau. of Francis and Jane Dade, May 14, 1718.
D. Francis Dade, Junr: Dec. 3, 1725.
D. Behethland Dade, Jan. 19, 1725/6.
M. Henry Dade and Elizabeth Massey, July 7, 1726.
B. Frances, dau. of Townshend and Elizabeth Dade, Aug. 30, 1726.
B. Mary, dau. of Henry and Elizabeth Dade, June 11, 1727.
B. Horatio, son of Townshend and Elizabeth Dade, 1729 (?1724)
B. Robert, son of Henry and Elizabeth Dade, May 14, 1731.
B. Frances Townshend, dau. of Townshend and Elizabeth Dade, Oct. 7, 1732.
B. Frances, dau. of Henry Dade, Mar. 12, 1733/4.
D. Elizabeth, wife of Henry Dade, Mar. 18, 1733/4.
B. Elizabeth, dau. of Townshend and Elizabeth Dade, Oct. 20, 1734.
D. Frances, dau. of Henry and Elizabeth Dade, Mar. 31, 1734.
M. Townshend Dade, Junr: and Parthenia Massey, May 6, 1736.
M. Baldwin Dade and Sarah Alexander, Aug. 7, 1736.
B. Cadwallader, son of Townshend and Elizabeth Dade, Dec. 26, 1736 and died
   soon after.
D. Elizabeth, wife of Townshend Dade, Dec. 30, 1736.
D. Cadwallader, son of Townshend and Elizabeth Dade, Dec. 30, 1736.
B. Anne Fowke, dau. of Townshend and Parthenia Dade, Dec. 13, 1737.
B. Francis, son of Baldwin and Sarah Dade, Dec. 29, 1737.
D. Sarah, wife of Baldwin Dade, Oct. 30, 1739.
M. Robert Dade and Elizabeth Harrison, Jan. 4, 1742/3.
M. Langhorne Dade and Mildred Washington, Feb. 14, 1742/3.
B. Townshend, son of Langhorne and Mildred Dade, Dec. 25, 1743.
D. Sarah, wife of Cadwallader Dade, Feb. 13, 1743/4.
D. Jane, wife of Francis Dade, May 23, 1744.
B. Behethland Alexander, dau. of Robert and Elizabeth Dade, Dec. 23, 1744
   and baptized Feb. 10, 1744/5.
M. Townshend Dade and Rose Grigsby, Dec. 12, 1745.
B. Cadwallader, son of Longhorne and Mildred Dade, Jan. 1, 1745/6.
M. Mary Dade and Howson Hooe, Junr: Sept. 26, 1746.
B. Sarah, dau. of Baldwin and Linny (?Verlinda) Dade, Jan. 20, 1746/7.
B. Jane, dau. of Langhorne and Mildred Dade, Apr. 2, 1748.
D. Jane, dau. of Langhorne and Mildred Dade, Sept. 28, 1748.
M. Horatio Dade and Frances Richards, Oct. 5, 1749.
M. Elizabeth Dade and Robert Yates, Feb. 17, 1750/1.
M. Elizabeth Dade and Lawrence Washington, July 31, 1751.
M. Cadwallader Dade and Sarah Berryman, Aug. 20, 1752.
M. Horatio Dade and Mary Massey, Jan. 14, 1753.
B. Franky, dau. of Horatio and Mary Dade, Oct. 10, 1753.
M. Frances Dade and Charles Stuart, Aug. 6, 1754.
M. Mildred Dade and (Dr.) Walter Williamson, Mar. 1, 1755.
M. Frances Dade and Francis Peyton, Apr. 24, 1755.
B. Horatio, son of Horatio and Mary Dade, Aug. 25, 1757.
B. Hannah Gibbons, dau. of Horatio and Mary Dade, July 1, 1759.
B. Baldwin, son of Baldwin and Verlinda Dade, Feb. 14, 1760.
B. Townshend, son of Cadwallader and Sarah Dade, Oct. 28, 1760.

M. Sarah Dade and Nehemiah Rodham Mason, Feb. 12, 1762.
B. Elizabeth, dau. of Baldwin and Verlinda Dade, June 13, 1764.
B. Townshend, son of Horatio and Mary Dade, June 3, 1766.
M. Townshend Dade and Jane Stuart, Dec. 11, 1769.
M. Anne Dade and Buckner Stith, Feb. 26, 1772.
M. Sarah Dade and Lawrence Taliaferro, Feb. 3, 1774.
M. Frances Dade and James Gwatkins, Mar. 25, 1774.
B. Townshend Stuart, son of Townshend and Jane Dade, Aug. 4, 1774.
D. Jane, wife of Townshend Dade and dau. of the Rev. William Stuart and
      Sarah, his wife, Aug. 10, 1774.
M. Jane Dade and Robert Yates, Apr. 11, 1777.
M. Behethland Dade and Justinian Birch, June 30, 1777.
M. Mary Dade and John Blaxton, Oct. 10, 1777.
M. Hannah Gibbons Dade and Lawrence Ashton, Feb. 1, 1779.
M. Elizabeth Dade and Townshend Dade, Aug. 5, 1782.
M. Sally Dade and James Park, Mar. 4, 1796.
M. Barbara Dagg and Samuel Sandys, Sept. 12, 1724.
M. John Dagg and Sarah Overall, Nov. 14, 1729.
B. Mary, dau. of John and Sarah Dagg, Jan. 3, 1730/1.
B. John, son of John and Sarah Dagg, Jan. 20, 1732/3.
B. William, son of John and Sarah Dagg, Feb. 20, 1734/5.
B. Sarah, dau. of John and Sarah Dagg, May 5, 1737.
B. Willoughby, son of Margaret Daking, Mar. 20, 1739/40.
M. Elizabeth Dalbin and William Jameson, Dec. 30, 1725.
D. Elizabeth Dalby, Jan. 25, 1727/8.
M. Richard Dane and Elizabeth Kelly, June 30, 1746.
M. Anne Darbin and Alexander Murphy, Apr. 8, 1724.
M. Mary Dart and John Fullager, Jan. 26, 1761.
M. Rachel Davies and William Embrey, Oct. 6, 1743.
B. Martha, dau. of Peter and Martha Davis, July 29, 1735.
D. Peter Davis, July 23, 1736.
M. Martha Davies and John Stone, May 16, 1739.
M. John Davis and Mary Branham, Sept. 8, 1745.
B. Anne, dau. of William and Isabel Davis, Oct. 23, 1745.
M. Rebecca Davis and Eli Stone, Dec. 4, 1746.
B. James, son of William and Isabella Davis, Apr. 17, 1747.
B. Isaac, son of John and Mary Davis, June 4, 1747.
M. John Davis and Sarah Hankins, Aug. 7, 1750.
B. William, son of William and Isabel Davis, June 14, 1751.
B. Elizabeth, dau. of John and Sarah Davis, Jan. 29, 1752.
M. William Davis and Sarah Franklin, May 13, 1752.
M. Martha Davis and William Mannard, Aug. 13, 1752.
M. Lucy, dau. of William and Ruth Davis, Aug. 26, 1757.
B. Abraham, son of Betty Davis, Mar. 3, 1758.
M. Henry Davis and Margaret Mills, Nov. 5, 1758.
B. Sarah, dau. of Thomas and Elizabeth Day, Aug. 22, 1726.
M. Elizabeth Day of Strother's Parish and Anthony Mislin, May 5, 1735.
M. Sarah Day and William Rose, June 6, 1737.
B. Francis, son of Elizabeth Day, Sept. 16, 1739.
M. Elizabeth Day and Samuel Crannidge, May 6, 1741.
M. Sarah Day of Hanover Parish and Charles Regg, July 17, 1746.
M. John Day and Behethland Bowling, Feb. 21, 1747/8.
M. John Day and Margaret Smith, May 15, 1758.
M. John Deacon and Mary Sacheveral, May 15, 1785.
M. Ambrose Deakins and Victory Sims, May 24, 1789.
D. Mary, dau. of Robert and Elizabeth Dearing, Sept. 7, 1717.

B. Jane, dau. of John and Mary Debell, May 3, 1735.
D. Abraham Delander, June 29, 1715.
M. Mary Delander and Patrick Morrow, Oct. 6, 1716.
M. Elinor Delander and Jacob Johnson, Dec. 10, 1728.
M. Mary Delander and Samuel Jackson, Feb. 21, 1736/7.
D. Abraham Delander, Oct. 25, 1740.
B. Winifred, dau. of Lydia Delisse, Dec. 7, 1768.
M. Mary Magdelene Delore (?) and John Whitcraft, Sept. 25, 1716.
M. John Demsoe and Jane Knight, July 6, 1737.
B. Anne, dau. of John and Jane Demsoe, June 9, 1738.
B. Elliott, dau. of John and Jane Demsoe, Aug. 5, 1740.
M. Thomas Dennett and Mary Horsey, June 18, 1758.
B. Margaret, dau. of Henry and Anne Dennis, Dec. 3, 1725.
D. Henry Dennis, Nov. 14, 1725.
M. Anne Dennis and Michael Price, Aug. 24, 1727.
M. William Dere and Sarah Head, Sept. 16, 1773.
D. Catherine, dau. of Matthew Derrick, Oct. 8, 1716.
B. Thomas, son of Maddox and Frances Derrick, Mar. 3, 1717/18.
B. Frances (?), dau. of Maddox and Frances Derrick, Aug.__, 1722.
M. Clary Derrick and Robert Mannard, May 27, 1723.
D. Frances, wife of Matthew Derrick, Jan. 12, 1725/6.
M. Edward Derrick and Jemima Powell, Jan. 2, 1728/9.
M. Benjamin Derrick and Mary Neale, Sept. 30, 1729.
B. Elizabeth, dau. of Edward and Jemima Derrick, Jan. 3, 1731/2.
M. Anne Derrick and Benoni Stratton, Dec. 24, 1733.
B. John, son of Edward and Jemima Derrick, Feb. 2, 1733/4.
B. Anne, dau. of Jane Derrick, July 20, 1734.
M. Benjamin Derrick and Margaret Cannady, Aug. 3, 1734.
D. Margaret Derrick, Dec. 2, 1734.
B. Thomas, son of Edward and Jemima Derrick, Apr. 2, 1736.
M. Benjamin Derrick and Katherine Powell, July 29, 1737.
B. Mary, dau. of Edward and Katherine Derrick, Sept. 30, 1737.
B. Jemima, dau. of Edward and Jemima Derrick, Mar. 6, 1738/9.
B. Behethland, dau. of Benjamin and Katherine Derrick, Sept. 6, 1739.
D. Edward Derrick, Apr. 27, 1741.
B. Benjamin, son of Benjamin and Katherine Derrick, June 3, 1741.
M. Jemima Derrick and John Thomas, Aug. 10, 1741.
M. Sarah Derrick and John Turner, Oct. 2, 1741.
B. Thomas, son of Benjamin and Katherine Derrick, Aug. 7, 1743.
B. Maddox, son of Benjamin and Katherine Derrick, Sept. 28, 1745.
D. Maddox Derrick, Jan. 8, 1745/6.
B. Edward, son of Benjamin and Katherine Derrick, Nov. 7, 1748.
B. John, son of Benjamin and Katherine Derrick, Sept. 18, 1750.
M. Elizabeth Derrick and William Stribling, Jan. 7, 1753.
B. Sarah, dau. of Benjamin and Katherine Derrick, Mar. 8, 1753.
M. William Derrick and Esther Jordan, Dec. 20, 1762.
M. Benjamin Derrick and Martha Whiting, Jan. 31, 1763.
B. Mary, dau. of Benjamin and Martha Derrick, Jan. 27, 1766.
M. Martha Derrick and John Turner, Sept. 2, 1769.
M. Phoebe Derrick and Charles Clark, Dec. 14, 1785.
M. John Devean and Mary Bridges of Overwharton Parish, Aug. 4, 1764.
M. Margaret Dew and William Kelly, Apr. 24, 1732.
M. William Dick and Sarah Lloyd, July 25, 1732.
M. Susanna Dickerson and James Barber, Sept. 25, 1779.
M. Jane Dinsford and Duncan Simpson, Dec. 27, 1732.
M. Anne Dishman of Washington Parish and Thomas Grigsby of Overwharton Parish
       Nov. 25, 1729.

M. John Diskins and Elizabeth Clark, Apr. 2, 1724.
B. William, son of Peter and Elizabeth Dixon, Jan. 12, 1717/8.
M. Richard Dixon and Anne Ramsey, Apr. 13, 1775.
M. Molly Dodd and John Bushell, Dec. 18, 1791.
M. Bushrod Doggett of Brunswick Parish and Anne Stribling of this parish, Oct. 6, 1737.
M. Elizabeth Doggett and John Carver, Aug. 31, 1757.
M. Anne Donahoo and John Hammit, Aug. 15, 1757.
M. Sarah Doniphan and William Hansford, Feb. 12, 1725/6.
M. Joseph Doody (Moody?) and Rachel Bowling, Feb. 13, 1750/1.
B. Henry, son of Thomas and Margaret Douglas, Mar. 25, 1738.
B. Frances, son of Joseph and Rachel Doody (Moody?), June 10, 1751.
B. Mary, dau. of Thomas and Margaret Douglas, Apr. 10, 1740.
M. Alexander Douglas and Keziah Riggins, May 21, 1749.
M. Elizabeth Douglas and Joseph Burgess, July 15, 1749.
B. William, son of Alexander and Keziah Douglas, July 16, 1750.
M. Alexander Douglas and Sarah Martin, Sept. 8, 1751.
B. Thomas, son of Alexander and Sarah Douglas, Aug. 9, 1752.
B. John, son of Alexander and Keziah Douglas, Oct. 14, 1752.
B. John, son of Alexander and Keziah Douglas, Mar. 15, 1756.
B. Anne, dau. of Alexander and Keziah Douglas, Oct. 24, 1757.
B. Jane, dau. of Alexander and Keziah Douglas, Jan. 17, 1761.
M. John Douling and Lettice Speerman of Washington Parish, May 1, 1746.
M. Grace Dounton and James Seaton, Mar. 11, 1730/1.
B. Anne, dau. of Mildred Dounton, Mar. 3, 1759.
M. Frances Dounton and John Johnson, July 30, 1778.
M. Sarah Dreem and Henry Locke, Sept. 17, 1722.
M. Andrew Drummond and Elizabeth Briscoe, Jan. 16, 1735/6.
B. Margaret, dau. of Andrew and Elizabeth Drummond, June 6, 1737.
B. James, son of Andrew and Elizabeth Drummond, мar. 12, 1738/9.
M. Leila Drummond and Henry Duval Manjeur, Apr. 30, 1758.
M. Elizabeth Gray Dudley and John Christie, Oct. 7, 1785.
B. James, son of James and Mary Duff, Apr. 5, 1762.
B. Judith, dau. of Susanna Duke, Dec. 12, 1742.
M. Judith Duke and Jeremiah Payne, May 25, 1760.
D. Peter Dukson, Mate of the Ship Exchange, Sept. 2, 1738.
M. Edward Dulaney and Mary Campbell, Apr. 15, 1726.
M. Mildred Duling and William Spillman, Dec. 22, 1787.
M. Verlinda Dunahoo and John Taylor, Dec. 13, 1776.
M. John Dunbar and Elizabeth Elliott, Sept. 26, 1752.
B. Susan, dau. of John and Elizabeth Dunbar, Mar. 23, 1755.
M. Mary Duncan and John Smith, Nov. 15, 1722.
M. Seely Duncan and Patrick Johnson, Nov. 17, 1724.
M. John Duncan and Lettice Woaker (?Walker) Sept. 27, 1735.
B. Thomas, son of John and Lettice Duncan, July 5, 1736.
B. Rose, dau. of Thomas and Sarah Duncomb, May 16, 1726.
B. Benjamin, son of Thomas and Mary Duncomb, Nov. 10, 1721.
M. Joyce Duncomb and Richard Bennett, Sept. 21, 1729.
M. Elizabeth Duncomb and Thomas Norman, Feb. 21, 1736/7.
D. John, son of Thomas Duncomb, Sept. 1, 1740.
D. Mary, wife of Thomas Duncomb, Dec. 8, 1741.
M. Mildred Duncomb and William Williams, Dec. 8, 1743.
D. Thomas Duncomb, Mar. 17, 1742/3.
B. John, son of Benjamin Duncomb by Sarah Prestridge, Dec. 28, 1748 (?1747).
M. Rosamond Duncomb and Thomas Carver, Aug. 12, 1755.
M. Thomas Duncomb and Sarah Whiting, June 2, 1758.

M. Eleanor Dunfee and Edward Oxives, Nov. 27, 1724.
M. Joseph Dunman of Washington Parish and Honor Bowling of this Parish, Jan. 4, 1726/7.
D. John Dunkirk, Apr. 2, 1726.
B. James, son of Mary Dunlop, Aug. 6, 1735.
B. Charlotte, dau. of Lydia Dunlop, Apr. 18, 1773.
D. Mary Dunn, Dec. 23, 1734.
B. Rose, dau. of Thomas and Mary Dunworth, May 16, 1726.
B. Mealy, son of Samuel and Mary Durham, Mar. 20, 1716/17 and baptized Mar. 24.
B. Sarah, dau. of Samuel and Mary Durham, Oct. 13, 1717.
B. Edward, son of Samuel and Mary Durham, Sept. 2, 1725.
M. Helen Durham and Robert Reddish, Nov. 10, 1727.
B. Frances, dau. of Samuel and Mary Durham, Feb. 24, 1727/8.
D. Samuel Durham, Nov. 23, 1735.
B. Jane, dau. of William and Margaret Durham, Oct. 2, 1739.
M. Matthew Dyall and Jane Wood, Jan. 23, 1738/9.
B. Reuben, son of Avery Dye, Mar. 27, 1749.
B. Mary, dau. of William and Elizabeth Dye, Dec. 5, 1753.
M. George Dye and Rebecca Dye, Mar. 10, 1790.
M. Rawleigh Dye and Parthenia Posey, May 7, 1790.

E

B. Sarah, dau. of Jonathan and Jane Eaton, Apr. 28, 1726.
M. Frances Eaton and Thomas Fleming, Apr. 10, 1735.
B. William, son of Elizabeth Eaton, May 20, 1735.
M. William Eaton and Mary Bowling, Aug. 25, 1737.[16]
B. Katherine, dau. of Sarah Edgar, Mar. 7, 1745/6.
M. John Edison (?Addison) and Anne Stratton, July 12, 1751.
M. Sarah Edrington of Sittingbourne Parish and Thomas Ammon, Jan. 24, 1733/4.
M. Nancy Edrington and William Ashmore, Jan. 14, 1781.
B. Haden, son of William and Mary Edwards, Washington Parish, Mar. 16, 1715/16.
M. Mary Edwards and (Thomas) Green, May 1, 1716.
M. Elizabeth Edwards and Patrick Ryan, May 6, 1723.
M. Hannah Edwards and Michael Summers, May 12, 1724.
M. Mary Edwards and Charles Wells, Dec. 10, 1733.
B. Jemima, dau. of Mary Edwards, Mar. 4, 1736/7.
M. Mary Edwards and John Philips, Feb. 27, 1737/8.
M. Gustavus Elgin and Anne Sutherland, Mar. 26, 1793.
M. Margaret Elkins and James Stevens, June 21, 1727.
M. Joan Elkins and Bartholomew Rodman, June 24, 1727.
M. Priscilla Elkins and Benjamin Sebastian, Feb. 16, 1729/30.
D. Anne Elliott, June 22, 1725.
M. Anne Elliott and Nicholas Sebastian, Oct. 29, 1726.
M. George Elliott and Mary Adams, Apr. 26, 1728.
B. Thomas, son of George and Mary Elliott, Feb. 28, 1731/2.
D. Charles Elliott (?Ellett), Oct. 23, 1734.
B. Elizabeth, dau. of George and Mary Elliott, Oct. 20, 1734.
B. Katherine, dau. of George and Mary Elliott, Dec. 10, 1736.
D. Mary Elliott, July 24, 1738.
B. Jane, dau. of George and Mary Elliott, Dec. 20, 1738.
B. Joseph, son of George and Mary Elliott, May 22, 1740.
B. George, son of George and Mary Elliott, Mar. 31, 1742.
B. Anne, dau. of George and Mary Elliott, July 17, 1743.

B. William Adams, son of George and Mary Elliott, Nov. 17, 1744.
D. Doctor Robert Elliott, Mar. 20, 1743/4.
B. Charles, son of George and Mary Elliott, Oct. 6, 1746.
M. Mary Elliott and Thomas Skinner, Dec. 26, 1749.
M. Sarah Elliott and Absolom Sudduth, Oct. 2, 1750.
M. Elizabeth Elliott and John Dunbar, Sept. 26, 1752.
M. William Elliott and Sarah Sharpe, Dec. 17, 1752.
M. John Ellis and Mary Oneal, Sept. 17, 1722.
M. Mary Ellis and John Overall, Oct. 8, 1722.
D. Sarah Ellis, Jan. 19, 1725/6.
M. Mary Ellis and John Harrod, Aug. 4, 1728.
B. Elizabeth, dau. of William and Anne Embrie, Nov. 22, 1726.
M. William Embry and Rachel Davies, Oct. 6, 1743.
B. Eli, son of William and Rachel Embry, Apr. 8, 1745.
D. John Embry, Oct. 5, 1746.
B. John, son of William and Rachel Embry, July 26, 1748.
M. Frances Embry and Thomas Elliott Sebastian, June 4, 1751.
M. Elizabeth Embry and James Sims, Oct. 14, 1762.
M. Thomas Emerson and Anne McKey, Apr. 17, 1743.
M. John Engles and Lettice Burgess, Feb. 15, 1736/7.
B. Sarah, dau. of Robert and Jane Engles, Nov. 4, 1737.
B. Sarah, dau. of John and Lettice Engles, Feb. 1, 1737/8.
B. Lettice, dau. of John and Lettice Engles, Aug. 8, 1739.
B. John, son of John and Lettice Engles, Feb. 1, 1740/1.
B. Margaret, dau. of John and Lettice Engles, June 24, 1743.
B. Anne, dau. of John and Lettice Engles, Oct. 12, 1745.
B. Sarah, dau. of John and Lettice Engles, July 24, 1748.
B. Letty, dau. of John and Lettice Engles, Feb. 23, 1750/1.
B. John, son of John and Lettice Engles, June 3, 1752.
B. Lettice, dau. of John (and Lettice?) Engles, Oct. 20, 1753.
B. Robert, son of John and Lettice Engles, July 25, 1756.
B. William, son of John and Lettice Engles, May 7, 1759.[17]
D. Robert English, Dec. 3, 1732.
D. Thomas Ennis, a servant boy, Sept. 16, 1721.
M. Elizabeth Evans of this Parish and Patrick Matthews of Nanjemoy Parish, Aug. 17, 1725.
M. Samuel Evans and Jane Riggins, June 29, 1746.
B. John, son of Samuel and Jane Evans, Dec. 18, 1746.
M. Thomas Evans and Anne Lucas, Feb. 4, 1753.
B. Sarah, dau. of Thomas and Anne Evans, Jan. 17, 1754.
M. Jane Evans and Matthew (?) Friar, Dec. 1, 1769.
M. Bethea Evans and Thomas Mehorner, Mar. 30, 1786.

F

B. Dennis, son of Martin and Mary Farrell, Sept. 27, 1742.
B. William, son of Martin and Mary Farrell, Apr. 27, 1745.
M. Elizabeth Fawyn (?Fruyn) and Edward Clement, Oct. 25, 1728.
M. John Fendall and Sarah Alexander, Sept. 24, 1751.
M. Peter Fernandis and Mildred Gooly, July 29, 1792.
M. John Fewel and Mary Grigsby, Oct. 14, 1726.
M. Sarah Fewel and Joseph Lee, July 22, 1792.
M. Ruth Finchum and John Pimm (?Primm), Dec. 29, 1760.
B. Jane, dau. of Daniel and Margaret Fingleston, Feb. 26, 1737/8.
B. Margaret, dau. of Daniel and Margaret Fingleston, Nov. 3, 1742.
B. Lettice, dau. of Daniel and Margaret Fingleston, Sept. 25, 1744.

M. Daniel Fingleston and Martha Whiting, Feb. 10, 1755.
M. Jane Fingleston and Robert Rankins, Dec. 26, 1756.
B. Robert, son of Mary Fingleston, Aug. 14, 1760.
M. Mary Anne Fingleston and John Addison, Apr. 17, 1761.
B. William, son of John and Anna Barbara Fitzhugh, Apr. 13, 1725.[18]
B. Thomas, son of Henry and Susanna Fitzhugh, July 16, 1725.
B. Sarah, dau. of Major John and Anna Barbara Fitzhugh, Apr. 30, 1727.
B. John, son of Henry and Susanna Fitzhugh, June 14, 1727.
B. John (?), son of John and Anna Barbara Fitzhugh, Jan. 4, 1729/30.
B. Betty, dau. of Col. Henry and Lucy Fitzhugh, Apr. 20, 1731.[19]
B. William and Sarah, son and dau. of Henry and Susanna Fitzhugh, Aug. 21, 1729.
B. Susanna, dau. of Capt. Henry and Susanna Fitzhugh, Sept. 19, 1732.
D. Major John Fitzhugh, Jan. 21, 1732/3.
B. Daniel, son of Major John (dec'd.?) and Anna Barbara Fitzhugh, June 27, 1733.
B. Anne, dau. of Col. Henry and Lucy Fitzhugh, Mar. 26, 1734.
M. Elizabeth Fitzhugh and Nathaniel Gray, Aug. 12, 1734.
M. Sarah Fitzhugh and Edward Barradoll, Jan. 5, 1735/6.
B. Elizabeth, dau. of Capt. Henry and Susanna Fitzhugh, Aug. 23, 1736.
B. Lucy, dau. of Col. Henry and Lucy Fitzhugh, Oct. 26, 1736.
M. Barbara Fitzhugh of this Parish and the Reverend Mr. William McKay, Rector of Hanover Parish, Feb. 6, 1738/9.
D. Anne, dau. of Col. Henry Fitzhugh, Oct. 1, 1739.
D. Lucy, dau. of Col. Henry Fitzhugh, Oct. 7, 1739.
M. Anne Fitzhugh of this Parish and the Rev. Robert Rose of St. Anne's Parish, Nov. 6, 1740.
M. Anne Fitzhugh and William Allison, Nov. 21, 1740.
B. William, son of Col. Henry and Lucy Fitzhugh, Aug. 24, 1741.
D. Colonel Henry Fitzhugh, Dec. 6, 1742.
M. Betty Fitzhugh and Benjamin Grymes, Feb. 12, 1746/7.
M. Sarah Fitzhugh and Francis Thornton, Apr. 2, 1747.
M. Thomas Fitzhugh and Sarah Stuart, June 19, 1750.
B. George, son of Col. Henry and Sarah Fitzhugh, Jan. 15, 1756.
B. William Beverley, son of William and Ursula Fitzhugh, Mar. 27, 1756.[20]
M. Elizabeth Fitzhugh and William Thornton, Apr. 26, 1757.
B. Daniel, son of William and Ursula Fitzhugh, Mar. 15, 1758.
M. John Fitzhugh and Elizabeth Harrison, Jan. 31, 1760.
B. Theodorick, son of William and Ursula Fitzhugh, July 2, 1760.
B. Thomas, son of Henry and Sarah Fitzhugh, Mar. 1, 1762.
M. Susanna Fitzhugh and Anthony Thornton, Jan. 5, 1764.
B. Nicholas Battalle, son of Henry and Sarah Fitzhugh, May 10, 1764.
B. Philip, son of William and Ursula Fitzhugh, May 4, 1766.
M. Henry Fitzhugh and Elizabeth Stith, Oct. 28, 1770.
M. Daniel Fitzhugh and Susanna Potter, Oct. 24, 1772.
M. Sarah Fitzhugh and Theodorick Bland, Dec. 5, 1772.
M. Elizabeth Fitzhugh and Henry Fitzhugh, Oct. 24, 1777.
M. Henry Fitzhugh and Elizabeth Fitzhugh, Oct. 24, 1777.
M. Lucy Fitzhugh and Alexander Campbell, Dec. 3, 1788.
M. Susannah Fitzhugh and Rice Wingfield Hooe, May 13, 1790.
M. Jane Fitzhugh and Henry Dade Hooe, June 17, 1790.
D. Mary, dau. of Rebecca Flagg, June 14, 1720.
D. William Flagg, Jan. 3, 1720/1.
M. Jane Flagg and Samuel King, Nov. 11, 1729.
M. Thomas Fleming and Frances Eaton, Apr. 10, 1735.
B. Elizabeth, dau. of Thomas and Frances Fleming, Dec. 15, 1735.

B. Sarah, dau. of Thomas and Frances Fleming, Mar. 18, 1736/7.
M. Thomas Fletcher and Mary Knight, Mar. 2, 1742/3.
M. Thomas Fletcher and Margaret Sherer, Dec. 26, 1744.
M. James Fletcher and Rachel Sebastian, Apr. 21, 1745.[21]
B. Thomas, son of Thomas and Margaret Fletcher, Dec. 20, 1745.
M. Francis Fletcher and Lettice Spicer, Nov. 8, 1745.
B. James, son of James and Rachel Fletcher, June 18, 1746.
B. Mary, dau. of Francis and Lettice Fletcher, Aug. 21, 1746.
B. Anne, dau. of James and Rachel Fletcher, Aug. 26, 1748.
B. Elizabeth, dau. of James and Rachel Fletcher, Mar. 8, 1752.
M. Thomas Fletcher and Margaret Hogsdale, Mar. 29, 1752.
M. Thomas Fletcher and Mary Jones, Dec. 28, 1753.
B. Mary, dau. of Thomas and Mary Fletcher, Jan. 25, 1754.
M. William Fletcher and Mary Grigsby, June 20, 1764.
B. John Story, son of John and Margaret Flower, Jan. 6, 1760.
B. Mary, dau. of John and Elizabeth Flower, Aug. 2, 1765.
M. Priscilla Flower and Alexander White, Apr. 30, 1775.
M. Jasper Floyd (Lloyd?) and Anne Chambers, Jan. 7, 1717/18.
M. Jasper Floyd and Elizabeth Cooper, Dec. 4, 1723.
B. James, son of Jasper and Elizabeth Floyd, Aug. 15, 1725.
B. Richard, son of Jasper and Elizabeth Floyd -- 1728.
B. Margaret, dau. of Jasper and Elizabeth Floyd, Nov. 13, 1732.
B. John, son of Anne Floyd, May 17, 1742.
D. Jasper Floyd, Nov. 20, 1743.
M. Anne Floyd and Thomas Williams, Dec. 23, 1744.
M. James Floyd and Margaret Lee, Feb. 20, 1749/50.
M. Anne Folly and Benjamin Grigsby, Sept. 5, 1727.
D. Richard Foote, Mar. 21, 1724/5.
D. Elizabeth Foote, Apr. 1, 1725.
M. Richard Foote and Katherine Fossaker, Oct. 6, 1726.
M. Hester Foote and John Grant, Aug. 17, 1727.
B. William, son of Richard and Katherine Foote, Oct. 31, 1727.
D. William (?) Foote, June 7, 1729.
M. George Foote of this Parish and Frances Berryman of Washington Parish,
     Dec. 3, 1731.
B. Sarah, dau. of Richard and Katherine Foote, Jan. 29, 1732/3.
B. George, son of George and Frances Foote, Jan. 20, 1734/5.
B. John, son of Richard and Katherine Foote, Nov. 30, 1735.
B. Gilson, son of George and Frances Foote, Dec. 18, 1736.
B. Henry, son of Richard and Katherine Foote, Apr. 11, 1738.
B. Katherine, dau. of Richard and Katherine Foote, Nov. 24, 1740.
B. Richard (?), son of Richard and Katherine Foote, Oct. 3, 1743.
B. Elizabeth, dau. of Richard and Katherine Foote, Dec. 10, 1746.
B. George, son of Richard Foote, Mar. 6, 1749/50.
M. Sarah Foote, and William Stuart, Nov. 26, 1750.
B. Francis, son of Richard and Katherine Foote, Oct. 12, 1753.
M. Catherine Foote and Lawrence Washington, Oct. 5, 1774.
M. Richard Foote and Jane Stuart, Dec. 16, 1795.
M. John Ford and Elizabeth Thornton, Jan. 27, 1729/30.
B. Mary, dau. of John and Elizabeth Ford, Mar. 6, 1731/2.
M. Warriner Ford and Frances Seaton, July 24, 1740.
M. Katherine Fossaker and Richard Foote, Oct. 6, 1726.
M. Elizabeth Fountain and Simon Perry, Feb. 16, 1791.
B. Chandler, son of Chandler and Mary Fowke, Nov. 7, 1717.
B. Robert Dinwiddie, son of Gerard and Elizabeth Fowke, Sept. 20, 1746.
M. Anne Fowke and John Hooe, Mar. 14, 1755.

B. John, son of Gerard and Elizabeth Fowke, June 26, 1757.
M. Richard Fowke and Anne Bunbury, Mar. 16, 1760.
B. Anne Harrison, dau. of Chandler and Mary Fowke, Sept. 13, 1760.[22]
B. Enfield, dau. of Gerard and Elizabeth Fowke, May 28, 1761.
B. Susanna, dau. of Richard and Anne Fowke, Dec. 6, 1761.
B. Frances, dau. of Chandler and Mary Fowke, May 15, 1762.
M. Susanna Fowke and Henry Peyton, Mar. 15, 1764.
B. George, son of Gerard and Elizabeth Fowke, Apr. 10, 1764.
B. Caty, dau. of Chandler and Mary Fowke, July 11, 1765.
B. Nelly, dau. of Chandler and Mary Fowke, Jan. 19, 1768.
B. Thomas Harrison, son of Chandler and Mary Fowke, June 1, 1770.
M. Judith Fowke and Enoch Berry, Nov. 23, 1791.
M. Alice Fowler of Brunswick Parish and George Williams, Dec. 31, 1734.
B. William, son of John and Elizabeth Fowler, Dec. 22, 1774.
B. Susanna, dau. of John and Elizabeth Fowler, Feb. 20, 1778.
B. Lucy, dau. of John and Elizabeth Fowler, May 19, 1782.
B. Augustus, son of John and Elizabeth Fowler, Jan. 22, 1785.
M. Sarah Fox and Richard Chidley, Dec. 21, 1722.
M. Helen Foy and John Conali, June 22, 1724.
D. Henry Francomb, Nov. 10, 1716.
D. John Frampton, a servant of Jeremy Crannedge, 14 of 7ber 1718.
D. Thomas Francomb, a servant, Jan. 16, 1719/20.
D. Elizabeth Francomb, Jan. 4, 1727/8.
M. William Francomb and Mary Kelly, June 22, 1728.
M. Sarah Frank and John Bailey, Jan. 6, 1745/6.
M. Elizabeth Frank of Washington Parish and John Kendall, Apr. 24, 1746.
M. John Franklin and Margaret Bolling, Aug. 18, 1716.
B. John, son of John and Margaret Franklin, Apr. 17, 1718.
B. John, son of John and Margaret Franklin, Aug. 16, 1720.[23]
B. Anne, dau. of Joseph and Sarah Franklin, Oct. 5, 1745.
M. Caesar Franklin and Sarah Kitchen, Aug. 28, 1746.
B. Polly, dau. of Caesar and Sarah Franklin, Aug. 29, 1747.
B. John, son of Joseph and Sarah Franklin, Jan. 18, 1747/8.
B. Winifred, dau. of Caesar and Sarah Franklin, Sept. 16, 1749.
B. Sally, dau. of Caesar and Sarah Franklin, Nov. 20, 1751.
M. Sarah Franklin and William Davis, May 13, 1752.
M. Samuel Franks and Parthenia Brown, Jan. 19, 1786.
M. Martin Frayn and Mary Anderson, July 9, 1758.
B. Mary, dau. of Thomas and Frances Freeman (Flecman?), Mar. 28, 1751.
B. Joseph, son of Thomas and Sarah Freeman, May 12, 1753.
M. Mason French and Margaret Lacy, Apr. 16, 1749.
M. John French and Margaret Burgess, Jan. 15, 1749/50.
M. Margaret French and Original Bowling, Mar. 18, 1752.
M. Matthew (?) Friar and Jane Evans, Dec. 1, 1769.
D. John Fruyn, Sept. 25, 1728.
M. Richard Fry and Margaret Hudson, July 11, 1745.
M. John Fullager and Mary Dart, Jan. 26, 1761.

G

M. Sarah Gardiner and Thomas Berry, Oct. 21, 1784.
M. Winifred Garmany and Ignatius Haddock, Oct. 20, 1729.
M. William Garrett and Anne Chambers, Jan. 28, 1717/8.
B. William and Jane, son and dau. of William and Anne Garrett, Oct. 2, 1718.
D. Anne Garrett, 1722.
M. Mary Garrett and John Hays, July 12, 1724.

D. Thomas Garrett, Oct. 18, 1735.
M. William Garrett and Sarah Awbry, Feb. 4, 1741/2.
B. John, son of William and Sarah Garrett, Mar. 14, 1745/6.
D. Sarah Garrett, May 3, 1748.
B. John, son of Anne Garrett, Oct. 26, 1748.
B. Daniel, son of Daniel and Elizabeth Garrett, Jan. 11, 1762.
B. Frances Clifton, dau. of Daniel and Elizabeth Garrett, Mar. 17, 1769.
B. Lewis, son of Nicholas and Martha George, Apr. 16, 1727.[24]
M. James Giles and Nancy Oliver, Mar. 24, 1788.
D. James Ginnis, May 20, 1718.
M. Jane Gladsteans and Peter Crafford, Aug. 7, 1755.
M. Thomas Glover and Sarah Kelly, Sept. 1, 1737.
B. John, son of Thomas and Sarah Glover, Dec. 9, 1738.
B. Mary, dau. of Thomas and Sarah Glover, Oct. 9, 1740.
B. Thomas, son of Thomas and Sarah Glover, Apr. 18, 1743.
M. Sarah Glover and John Christie, Aug. 28, 1743.
D. Thomas Glover, Nov. 22, 1743 (?1742).
M. William Goff and Maria Kelly, Sept. 8, 1738.
B. Frances, dau. of William and Anne (Maria?) Goff, Oct. 7, 1740.
M. Frances Goff and William Johnson, Nov. 20, 1762.
M. Margaret Golding and John Bedford, Aug. 8, 1729.
M. Thomas Golding and Frances Berry, Jan. 28, 1738/9.
B. Mary, dau. of Sarah Gooden, Jan. 19, 1741/2.
M. James Goodwin and Sarah Sawyer, June 5, 1735.
B. Barbara, dau. of James and Sarah Goodwin, Feb. 15, 1735/6.
B. Elizabeth, dau. of James and Sarah Goodwin, Jan. 10, 1739/40.
D. James Goodwin, Feb. 15, 1739/40.
M. Mildred Gooly and Peter Fernandis, July 29, 1792.
M. Alexander Gordon and Elizabeth (?Meredith), 1716.
M. John Gordon and Sarah Reddish, Jan. 24, 1722/3.
M. Eliza Gordon and Griffin Johns, Feb. 7, 1731/2.
M. Anne Gordon and John Oakley, Feb. 14, 1744/5.
M. John Gordon and Elizabeth Mustin, Nov. 24, 1747.
B. Thomas, son of John Gordon, Jan. 20, 1757.
B. William, son of John and Elizabeth Gordon, July 26, 1760.
B. George Meredith and Francis, son of John Gordon, July 17, 1765.
M. John Gordon Junr: and Margaret Rogers, Nov. 22, 1776.
M. Penelope Gorman and Robert Barber, Oct. 26, 1747.
M. Mary Gosling and Robert Crook, April 15, 1745.
B. Robert, son of Reuben Gosmack (Gormack?), Mar. 3, 1744/5.
M. Joseph Goss and Anne Joy, Dec. 24, 1747.
B. Henry, son of Joseph and Anne Goss, Oct. 27, 1761.
M. Henry Goss and Elizabeth Joy, Aug. 8, 1773.
M. Sophia Gotbey and John Coggins, Feb. 22, 1736/7.
M. Nancy Gouldie and John Whiting, Oct. 25, 1785.
M. Sarah Graham and John Bryant, Dec. 11, 1768.
M. John Grant and Hester Foote, Aug. 17, 1727.
D. Mary Grant, Nov. 22, 1728.
M. Andrew Grant and Mary Matthews, Apr. 26, 1770.
M. Anne Mary Grant and William Matthews, Dec. 5, 1781.
M. James Grant and Elizabeth Massey, Jan. 10, 1793.
B. William, son of John and Elizabeth Gravat, Jan. 31, 1731/2.
B. George, son of John and Elizabeth Gravat, July 26, 1733.
B. Katherine, dau. of John and Elizabeth Gravat, Jan. 6, 1736/7.
B. Elizabeth, dau. of John and Elizabeth Gravat, Feb. 7, 1739/40.
M. Elizabeth Gravat and James Mehorner, Feb. 7, 1742/3.

M. John Gravat and Behethland Kelly, Dec. 27, 1751.
B. Ursula, dau. of John and Behethland Gravat, June 10, 1752.
M. George Gravat and Catherine McCarty, May 9, 1756.
B. Ellis, son of George and Catherine Gravat, Mar. 21, 1757.
M. Behethland Gravat and Alexander Jordan, Oct. 30, 1758.
M. Elizabeth Gravat and Francis Selph, Oct. 16, 1763.
M. Ursula Gravat and William McDonald, July 1, 1767.
M. Nathaniel Gray and Elizabeth FitzHugh, Aug. 12, 1734.
B. John, son of Nathaniel and Elizabeth Gray, May 9, 1735.
B. Mary, dau. of Nathaniel and Elizabeth Gray, Nov. 1, 1736.
B. Nathaniel, son of Nathaniel and Elizabeth Gray, July 8, 1738.
B. Anna Barbara, dau. of Nathaniel and Elizabeth Gray, Sept. 19, 1739.
B. Winifred, dau. of Nathaniel and Elizabeth Gray, Oct. 5, 1741.
B. Nathaniel, son of Nathaniel and Elizabeth Gray, Apr. 6, 1744.
B. George, son of Nathaniel and Elizabeth Gray, Nov. 24, 1746 and died soon
   after.
B. Sarah, dau. of Nathaniel and Elizabeth Gray, Feb. 6, 1747/8.
B. John, son of Nathaniel and Elizabeth Gray, Apr. 25, 1750.
B. Margaret, dau. of Nathaniel and Elizabeth Gray, Feb. 24, 1752.
B. George, son of George and Sarah Gray, Aug. 10, 1756.25
B. James, son of George and Mary Gray, Jan. 22, 1758.
M. John Gray and Sarah Thomas, May 11, 1758.
B. Francis, son of George and Mary Gray, Oct. 22, 1759.
M. Winifred Gray and William Johnson, Feb. 24, 1760.
B. Daniel, son of George and Mary Gray, Dec. 9, 1761.
B. Elizabeth, dau. of John and Sarah Gray, Apr. 15, 1762.
B. Nathaniel Weedon, son of George and Mary Gray, Oct. 19, 1763.
M. Sarah Gray and William Scott, Apr. 18, 1765.
B. French, son of George Gray and Mary, Mar. 11, 1766.
B. Peggy Strother, dau. of George Gray, July 20, 1768.
M. (Thomas) Green and Mary Edwards, May 1, 1716.
M. Mary Green of Washington Parish and James Yates of Sittenbourne Parish,
   Nov. 19, 1745.
M. Thomas Green and Lydia Whitledge of Hamilton Parish, Mar. 29, 1746.
M. Martha Greenslet and Isaac Shepherd, Feb. 17, 1749/50.
M. Catherine Greenleves and Edward Morris (Morning?), Oct. 16, 1779.
B. Mary, dau. of George and Eleanor Gregg, Apr. 25, 1719.
B. George, son of George and Eleanor Gregg, Sept. 28, 1723.
B. Elizabeth, dau. of George and Eleanor Gregg, Apr. 24, 1728.
M. John-Ben Gregg and Sarah Smith, June 22, 1730.
D. Anne Gregg, Feb. 9, 1730/1.
B. Mary, dau. of John-Ben Gregg and Sarah his wife, July 16, 1733.
M. George Gregg and Jane Vincent, Feb. 5, 1734/5.
D. George Gregg, Oct. 23, 1735.
B. Merriday (?Meredith), son of John-Ben and Sarah Gregg, Dec. 27, 1735.
M. Jane Gregg and Edmund Kelly, June 15, 1736.
B. Sarah, dau. of John-Ben and Sarah Gregg, Jan. 6, 1736/7.
M. Elizabeth Gregg and Richard Vincent, Apr. 9, 1737.
B. Samuel, son of John-Ben and Sarah Gregg, May 6, 1739.
B. Isabel, dau. of Jane Gregg, Sept. 10, 1750.
B. George, son of George Gregg, Nov. 13, 1755.
M. Sarah Gregg and Charles Smith, Jan. 20, 1759.
M. William Griffin and Margaret Corbin, Apr. 6, 1725.
M. Elizabeth Griffin and James Berry, Aug. 19, 1747.
M. Sarah Griffin and James Newman, Dec. 25, 1759.
M. Anne Griffin and Thomas Zachary, Apr. 20, 1760.

M. Dully Griffin and John Acres, May 28, 1790.
B. Katherine, dau. of Francis and Mary Griffith, Dec. 1, 1726.
B. John, son of Francis and Mary Griffith, Oct. 30, 1731.
B. Mary Anne, dau. of Richard and Jane Griffith, Dec. 21, 1755.
M. Mary Griffith and George Nailour Wassle, July 26, 1792.
M. Elizabeth Griggs and William Young, Aug. 29, 1746.
M. George Griggs and Margaret Humphries, June 22, 1749.
B. Eleanor, dau. of George and Margaret Griggs, Mar. 5, 1749/50.
B. John, son of George and Margaret Griggs, Aug. 25, 1751.
M. Elizabeth Griggs and John Christie, Sept. 12, 1751.
B. George, son of George and Jane (?) Griggs, Nov. 13, 1755.
B. Sarah, dau. of George and Margaret Griggs, Aug. 5, 1760.
B. Eleanor, dau. of George and Margaret Griggs, Mar. 5, 1758.
M. Anne Griggs and Charles Smith, Jan. 24, 1769.
M. Mary Griggs and Lewis Knowland, Mar. 26, 1771.
M. Mary Grigsby and John Fewel, Oct. 14, 1726.
M. Benjamin Grigsby and Anne Foley (?), Sept. 5, 1727.
M. Margaret Grigsby and John Smith, Nov. 5, 1728.[26]
D. John Grigsby supposed to be 107 years old, Oct. 11, 1730.
M. Thomas Grigsby of Overwharton Parish and Anne Dishman of Washington
      Parish, Nov. 25, 1729.
M. Rose Grigsby and Benjamin Spicer, June 6, 1734.
M. James Grigsby and Sarah Sudduth, May 9, 1742.
M. Moses Grigsby of Overwharton Parish and Katherine Branson, Dec. 1, 1742.
B. Elizabeth, dau. of James and Sarah Grigsby, Feb. 24, 1742/3.
D. Thomas Grigsby, May 7, 1745.
M. Rose Grigsby and Townshend Dade, Dec. 12, 1745.
M. Rachel Grigsby and Isaac Rose, Dec. 19, 1751.
M. Susannah Grigsby and Charles Stuart of King Geo. County, Nov. 9, 1752.
M. James Grigsby and Letitia Travers, Jan. 18, 1753.[27]
B. John, son of James and Sarah Grigsby, Aug. 7, 1757.
M. Anne Grigsby and Samuel Grigsby, Dec. 25, 1762.
M. Samuel Grigsby and Anne Grigsby, Dec. 25, 1762.
M. Mary Anne Grigsby and John Markous, Sept. 1, 1763.
M. Mary Grigsby and William Fletcher, June 30, 1764.
M. Jemima Grining and Stephen Cash, May 26, 1747.
M. James Grisset and Elizabeth Philips, May 19, 1791.
M. Benjamin Grymes and Betty Fitzhugh, Feb. 12, 1746/7.
B. Benjamin, son of Benjamin and Betty Grymes, Jan. 2, 1756.
M. Mary Grymes and William Randolph, May 18, 1770.
D. Elizabeth Gurley, Nov. 10, 1726.
M. Anne Gutridge and Henry Smith, July 17, 1778.
M. Thomas Gutridge and Sarah Rawlings, May 16, 1782.
M. James Gwatkins and Frances Dade, Mar. 25, 1774.

H

M. Ignatius Haddock and Winifred Garmany, Oct. 20, 1729.
B. Margaret, dau. of Ignatius and Winifred Haddock, Feb. 10, 1731/2.
D. John Hadsworth, Mar. 18, 1742/3.
M. Elizabeth Hair and Thomas Hawkins, July 24, 1716.
D. Anne, dau. of Mary Hall, Oct. 6, 1717.
B. Sarah, dau. of James and Catherine Hall, May 1, 1723.
M. Joseph Hall and Mary Barron, Oct. 13, 1727.
Bapt: Sarah, dau. of Joseph Hall and Mary Barron, Nov. 8, 1725.
B. Catherine, dau. of James and Catherine Hall, June 3, 1726.

B. Billie, son of Elizabeth Hall, Dec. 25, 1734.
D. Mary Hall, Jan. 31, 1735/6.
D. Joseph Hall, Feb. 9, 1735/6.
B. Frances, dau. of Bathsheba Hall, Apr. 26, 1742.
B. Anne, dau. of Bathsheba Hall, Apr. 11, 1744.
M. Michael Hall and Elizabeth Kelly, Dec. 29, 1744.
M. Bathsheba Hall, and Samuel McKie, Mar. 4, 1744/5.
M. John Hall and Hannah Sudduth, Nov. 6, 1749.
M. Sarah Hall and Samuel Whiting, Oct. 5, 1750.
B. Benjamin, son of John and Hannah Hall, Nov. 14, 1751.
B. Anne, dau. of John and Hannah Hall, Aug. 4, 1754.
B. Butral, dau. of Futral and Elizabeth Hall, Apr. 14, 1760.[28]
B. Hannah, dau. of Frances Hall, Feb. 14, 1764.
M. John Hallett and Mary Walker, Aug. 1, 1751.
D. Thomas Halsall, Commander of the Liverpool Merchant, Sept. 25, 1738.
M. Margaret Hamilton and William Norton, Feb. 26, 1724/5.
M. Thomison Hamm and William Thomas, Dec. 22, 1724.
M. Sarah Hamm and William Barton, Dec. 1, 1730.
D. John Hamm, Dec. 8, 1739.
M. Daniel Hammit and Bethridge Bowling, Nov. 2, 1728.
B. Verlinda, dau. of Daniel and Elizabeth Hammit, Jan. 6, 1738/9.
B. Elizabeth, dau. of Daniel and Elizabeth Hammit, July 22, 1742.
B. Mildred, dau. of Daniel and Elizabeth Hammit, Apr. 25, 1745.
M. John Hammit and Anne Donahoo, Aug. 15, 1757.
B. Mildred, dau. of David and Mildred (Hammit?), June 30, 1771.
B. George, son of Mildred Hammit, Apr. 12, 1773.
M. Daniel Hammit and Eleanor Jones, Dec. 22, 1774.
M. Anne Hammit and Zachariah Newble, Nov. 6, 1779.
B. Elizabeth, dau. of John and Mary Hammond, Oct. 12, 1772.
D. Joseph Hampton, Feb. 20, 1725/6.
M. Bryant Handley and Sarah Williams, Dec. 28, 1726 (sic).
B. Bridget, dau. of Bryant and Sarah Handley, Oct. 24, 1724.
D. Bridget Handley, Nov. 15, 1725.
M. Benjamin Handley (Hansley?) and Elizabeth Hickum, Jan. 19, 1730/1.
B. John, son of Bryant and Sarah Handley, July 20, 1732.
D. Bryant Handley, Dec. 20, 1732.
M. Sarah Handley and Benjamin Lewis, Aug. 31, 1734.
M. Margaret Handley and Francis Mills, Apr. 6, 1751.
B. John, son of Rachel Handy, Sept. 24, 1746.
M. Sarah Hankins, and John Davis, Aug. 7, 1750.
D. Rebecca Hannidge, Dec. 29, 1720.
B. Thomas, son of George and Elizabeth Hannidge, July 13, 1724.
D. Elizabeth, wife of George Hannidge, Dec. 25, 1744.
B. Elizabeth, dau. of Thomas and Jane Hannidge, Oct. 18, 1746.
B. Eleanor, dau. of Thomas and Jane Hannidge, Aug. 22, 1748.
M. James Hansbury and Lettice Summers, Sept. 19, 1741.
B. Mary, dau. of James Hansbury, Feb. 8, 1764. OVERWHARTON.
M. William Hansford and Sarah Doniphon, Feb. 12, 1725/6.
M. George Hardin and Jane Bunbury, Dec. 3, 1740.
M. Solomon Hardwick and Anne Beach, Sept. 25, 1748.
M. John Harges and Elizabeth Sublinel, Oct. 1, 1725.
B. Mildred, dau. of John and Elizabeth Harges, Aug. 4, 1726.
M. Richard Harmon and Elizabeth Mizing, Mar. 28, 1746.
M. George Harris and Mary Carroll, July 14, 1750.
M. Elizabeth Harrison and Robert Dade, Jan. 4, 1742/3.
M. Mary Harrison and George Catlett, Nov. 23, 1758.

M. Elizabeth Harrison and John Fitzhugh, Jan. 3, 1760.
M. Benjamin Harrison and Mary Short, Nov. 17, 1770.
M. John Harrod and Mary Ellis, Aug. 4, 1728.
M. James Hartley and Mary Kelly, Aug. 25, 1754.
M. James Hartley and Elizabeth Tilcock, Apr. 1, 1768.
M. James Hartley and Anne Walpole, Aug. 26, 1778.
M. Anne Hartley and Simon Perry, Dec. 25, 1783.
B. Anne, dau. of Edward and Mary (Harvey?), May 22, 1717.
M. Thomas Hawkins and Elizabeth Hair, July 24, 1716.
D. John Hawkins, Nov. 20, 1717.
D. Christian Hawkins, Nov. 6, 1721.
M. William Hawkins and Rose Cooke, Aug. 16, 1723.
D. Elizabeth Hawkins, June 30, 1726.
B. William, son of William and Rose Hawkins, Oct. 3, 1727.
D. William Hawkins, Sept. 14, 1734.
D. Thomas Hawkins, Jan. 10, 1735/6.
M. Thomas Hawkins and Sarah Ancrum, July 13, 1746.
B. William, son of Thomas and Sarah Hawkins, Apr. 17, 1747.
M. Mary Haydon and Peter Kilgore, Nov. 1, 1722.
M. John Haynes and Margaret Lindsay, Sept. 8, 1728.
M. John Hay and Mary Garrett, July 12, 1724.
B. Sarah, dau. of John and Mary Hay, May 19, 1725.
D. Sarah, dau. of John and Mary Hay, Sept. 6, 1725.
B. Margaret, dau. of John and Mary Hay, Oct. 18, 1732.
M. Sarah Head and William Dere, Sept. 16, 1773.
B. Elizabeth, dau. of Thomas and Mary Heath, June 9, 1716.
B. Luke, dau. of Rose Heath, Apr. 4, 1740.
B. George, son of Peter and Margaret Hedgman, Dec. 11, 1735.[29]
M. John Heneage and Molly Sparkes, Oct. 22, 1785.
B. Winifred, dau. of Enoch and Elizabeth Hensley, Feb. 25, 1752.
M. William Henson and Susanna Roth, Nov. 19, 1725.
B. Robert, son of Osman and Alse Henvigh, Mar. 3, 1715/16.
M. William Heselton and Hannah Leonard, July 7, 1765.
M. George Hibbill (? Hill) and Mary Triplett, Feb. 12, 1728/9.
M. Elizabeth Hickum and Benjamin Handley (Hansley?), Jan. 19, 1730/1.
B. Lydia, dau. of John and Sarah Hickum, Nov. 24, 1768.
M. Nathaniel Higdon (Hogdon?) and Margaret Oliver, Mar. 2, 1746/7.
B. John, son of James and Catherine Higgins, May 17, 1716.
B. Jane, dau. of James and Catherine Higgins, Dec. 4, 1719.
M. William Higgins and Sarah Newton, Dec. 9, 1732.
M. John Hill and Elizabeth Mahoney, Oct. 1, 1716.
D. Elizabeth, dau. of John Hill, Sept. 6, 1716.
B. Anne, dau. of John and Elinor Hill, Dec. 25, 1717.
B. Mary, dau. of John and Elizabeth Hill, Feb. 22, 1727/8.
M. Mary Hill and William Clift, Jan. 19, 1730/1.
B. Sarah, dau. of John and Elizabeth Hill, Jan. 24, 1730/1.
M. Frances Hill and Burdet Clifton, July 15, 1733.
B. Peggy, dau. of John and Elizabeth Hill, Jan. 20, 1733/4.
M. Richard Hill and Sarah Burnsplat, Dec. 22, 1737.
B. Isabel, dau. of Archibald and Eleanor Hodge, July 23, 1740.
B. Helen (Eleanor?), dau. of Archibald & Helen (?Eleanor) Hodge, Nov. 27, 1742.
M. Mary Hodge and Colclough Stripling, Oct. 6, 1749.
M. Eleanor Hodge and Clement Sacheveral, Nov. 8, 1763.
M. Isabel Hodge and Henry Buttridge, Dec. 30, 1764.
M. Margaret Hogsdale and Thomas Fletcher, Mar. 29, 1752.

B. Lilly, dau. of James and Mary Holdan, Mar. 8, 1759.
B. John, son of Tandy and Mary Holeman, July 14, 1731.
M. Elizabeth Holeman and Callehill Minnis, Nov. 16, 1740.
B. Anne, dau. of John and Anne Holland, May 12, 1752.
B. George, son of John and Elizabeth Holland, Feb. 17, 1757.
B. Elizabeth, dau. of John and Elizabeth Holland, May 6, 1759.
M. Jane Holland and William Thompson, Dec. 26, 1765.
M. Isabel Holland and Thomas Philips, June 14, 1772.
M. Elizabeth Holland and John Hudson, Aug. 24, 1780.
M. Mary Holland and John Mildred Scott, Feb. 26, 1784.
M. Anne Holloway and William Scapelan, Sept. 29, 1748.
B. Rice, son of Rice and Katherine Hooe, Mar. 14, 1724/5.[30]
D. Colonel Rice Hooe, Apr. 19, 1726.
D. Frances Hooe, Apr. 26, 1726.
M. Sarah Hooe and Philip Alexander, Nov. 11, 1726.
M. John Hooe and Anne Alexander, Nov. 23, 1726.
B. Richard, son of Rice and Katherine Hooe, Oct. 15, 1727.
B. John, son of Howson and Anne Hooe, Feb. 23, 1727/8.
D. Katherine Hooe, Nov. 8, 1731.
B. Gerard, son of John and Anne Hooe, Sept. 14, 1733.
B. Seymour, son of John and Anne Hooe, June 13, 1735.
B. Harris, son of Howson and Anne Hooe, Jan. 1, 1735/6.
B. John, son of John and Anne Hooe, Dec. 26, 1737.
B. Verlinda Harrison, dau. of Rice and Tabitha Hooe, Feb. 28, 1738/9.
B. Bernard, son of Howson and Anne Hooe, Oct. 30, 1739.
B. Anne, dau. of John and Anne Hooe, Dec. 7, 1739.
B. Joseph Harrison, son of Rice and Tabitha Hooe, Jan. 22, 1740/1.
B. Sarah, dau. of John and Anne Hooe, Mar. 7, 1741/2.
B. Mary Townshend, dau. of Rice and Tabitha Hooe, Feb. 27, 1741/2.
D. Parthenia, dau. of John and Anne Hooe, Aug. 26, 1742.
B. William, son of Howson and Anne Hooe, Sept. 19, 1743.
B. Robert Townshend, son of Rice and Tabitha Hooe, Oct. 3, 1743.
B. Sarah, dau. of Rice and Tabitha Hooe, June 20, 1746.
M. Howson Hooe, Junr: and Mary Dade, Sept. 26, 1746.
B. Henry Dade, son of Howson and Mary Hooe, June 9, 1747.
D. Mr. Rice Hooe, Jan. 22, 1747/8.
B. Robert Howson, son of Howson and Elizabeth Hooe, Nov. 22, 1748.
M. Frances Hooe and John Storke, Mar. 21, 1750/1.
M. John Hooe and Anne Fowke, Mar. 14, 1755.
B. Mary Anne, dau. of John Hooe, Junr: and Anne, Nov. 7, 1756.
B. Rice Wingfield, son of Richard and Anne Hooe, June 25, 1764.
M. Sarah Hooe and Nathaniel Washington, Dec. 17, 1767.
B. Sarah Barnes, dau. of Gerard and Sarah Hooe, June 5, 1769.[31]
M. Bernard Hooe and Margaret Pratt, Nov. 2, 1771.
M. Anne Hooe and William Allison, June 26, 1772.
M. Anne Hooe and Alvin Moxley, Nov. 5, 1772.
M. Seymour Hooe and Sarah Alexander, Mar. 9, 1776.
M. Susanna Hooe and Thomas Roy, Sept. 7, 1777.
B. Nathaniel Harris, son of William and Anne Hooe, Oct. 15, 1777.
B. Alexander Seymour, son of Seymour and Sarah Hooe, Dec. 15, 1777.
B. Jane Seymour, dau. of Seymour Hooe, Apr. 11, 1781.
M. Caty Hooe and William Winters, Nov. 1, 1781.
M. William Hooe and Susanna Pratt, Nov. 13, 1782.
M. Elizabeth Hooe and George Mason, Apr. 22, 1784.
M. Rice Wingfield Hooe and Susanna Fitzhugh, May 13, 1790.
M. Henry Dade Hooe and Jane Fitzhugh, June 17, 1790.

B. Hannah Fitzhugh, dau. of Rice W. Hooe and Sukey, his wife, Mar. 25, 1791.
D. William Hopkins, July 26, 1725.
B. Richard, son of Thomas Hornbuckle, Sept. 4, 1764.
B. John and William, sons of Hugh and Elizabeth Horton, Mar. 6, 1717/18.
M. Mary Horsey and Thomas Dennett, June 18, 1758.
M. William Horton of King George county and Mary Thornberry of St. Paul's Parish, Jan. 12, 1741/2.
M. Thomas Horton and Hannah Saunders, Feb. 10, 1786.
M. Sarah Howell and James McIntosh, Dec. 17, 1773.
B. Elizabeth, dau. of Edward and Elizabeth Hubbard, July 4, 1716.
M. Moses Hubbard and Sarah Lowry, Mar. 23, 1726/7.
B. Edward, son of Moses and Sarah Hubbard, Jan. 26, 1731/2.
M. Elizabeth Hubbard and James Bennett, Dec. 1, 1731.
B. Sebra, dau. of Moses and Sarah Hubbard, Feb. 2, 1733/4.
B. Moses, son of Moses and Sarah Hubbard, Mar. 18, 1735/6.
B. Sarah, dau. of Moses and Sarah Hubbard, Nov. 1, 1738.
M. Margaret Hubert and John Travis, June 28, 1722.
M. Mary Hudson and John Welch, Nov. 16, 1727.
M. Margaret Hudson and Richard Fry, July 11, 1745.
M. John Hudson and Elizabeth Holland, Aug. 24, 1780.
M. William Hudson and Margaret Rawlings, Mar. 10, 1785.
M. Mary Hudson and William Barrett, Dec. 30, 1785.
D. Timothy Hughes, Dec. 5, 1717.
D. Catherine, wife of Timothy Hughes, Dec. 7, 1717.
M. Luke Hughes and Behethland Kennedy, July 10, 1779.
B. John, son of John and Joyce Humphries, Feb. 19, 1716/7 and baptized Mar. 24:
B. William, son of John and Joyce Humphries, Dec. 5, 1720.
D. William, son of John and Joyce Humphries, July 15, 1725.
D. Joseph Humphreys, Jan. 22, 1725/6.
D. Katherine Humphreys, Jan. 23, 1725/6.
M. Margaret Humphries and George Griggs, June 22, 1749.
B. Samuel, son of William and Sarah Humphreys, Feb. 8, 1753.[32]
D. Mary Humstone, a child, Jan. 19, 1725/6.
D. William Humstone, Nov. 14, 1728.
D. Thomas Humstone, Dec. 1, 1730.
B. Thomas, son of Edward and Sarah Humstone, Mar. 17, 1731/2.
B. Anne, dau. of Edward and Sarah Humstone, Mar. 2, 1734/5.
B. Edward, son of Edward and Sarah Humstone, Sept. 22, 1737.
B. John, son of Edward and Sarah Humstone, Feb. 10, 1739/40.
B. Sarah, dau. of Edward and Sarah Humstone, May 2, 1743.
B. William, son of John and Frances Humstone, Jan. 10, 1744/5.
M. Thomas Hungerford and Anne Washington, June 22, 1780.
D. Susanna Hurdly, Feb. 9, 1725/6.
M. George Hutcheson and Mildred Wagstaff, Sept. 19, 1727.
B. William, son of George and Mildred (Hutcheson?) -- 1729.
B. Mildred, dau. of George and Mildred Hutcheson, June -- and baptized Aug. 5, 1731.
B. Jane, dau. of George and Mildred Hutcheson, Sept. 10, 1733.
D. George Hutcheson, Jan. 26, 1734/5.
M. Mildred Hutcheson and Hugh Carnady, Nov. 6, 1735.
M. Sarah Hutton and James Cullings, Feb. 14, 1755.
M. John Hyatt and Anne Lloyd, Jan. 7, 1717/8.

B. John, son of William and Mary Jackson, Oct. 28, 1716.
M. John Jackson and Rachel Rosser of Hanover Parish, Jan. 31, 1731/2.
M. Samuel Jackson and Mary Delander, Feb. 21, 1736/7.
B. James, son of Samuel and Mary Jackson, Aug. 14, 1738.
D. Mary, wife of Samuel Jackson, Dec. 1, 1739.
M. Samuel Jackson and Anne Berry, Feb. 10, 1739/40.
B. Samuel, son of Samuel and Anne Jackson, May 16, 1742.
D. Anne, wife of Samuel Jackson, Jan. 14, 1742/3.
D. Samuel Jackson, Feb. 14, 1747/8.
M. Elizabeth Jackson and Henry Smith, July 11, 1753.
M. Jane Jackson and Henry Bussey, Nov. 21, 1758.
M. James Jackson and Mary Johnson, Sept. 3, 1761.
B. Samuel, son of James and Mary Jackson, May 16, 1762.
M. Elizabeth Jackson and John Ashton, May 16, 1762.
M. James Jackson and Elizabeth Sweeny, Dec. 31, 1767.
B. Sarah, dau. of James and Elizabeth Jackson, Apr. 1, 1768.
B. Elizabeth, dau. of James and Elizabeth Jackson, Feb. 16, 1771.
B. Chandler, son of Samuel and Jane Jackson, Apr. 3, 1772.
B. Anne, dau. of Samuel and Jane Jackson, May 26, 1774.
M. John James and Anne Sebastian, Dec. 29, 1737.[33]
B. Samuel, son of John and Anne James, Nov. 19, 1738.
B. Sarah, dau. of John and Anne James, Apr. 9, 1746.
M. John James and Anne Strother, Sept. 16, 1763.
D. Sarah Jameson 5 of 7ber (Sept. 5) 1716.
M. William Jameson and Elizabeth Dalbin, Dec. 30, 1725.
B. Mary, dau. of William and Elizabeth Jameson, Oct. 15, 1726.
B. Jarvis, son of William and Elizabeth Jameson, Apr. 26, 1728.
B. Mary, dau. of William (and Elizabeth Jameson), --1729.
M. David Jameson and Jane Sebastian, May 7, 1744.
M. Thomas Jett and Lucinda Owens, Jan. 12, 1775.
M. Griffin Johns and Eliza Gordon, Feb. 7, 1731/2.
M. Margaret Johns and John Clift, Mar. 2, 1738/9.
D. Sarah, dau. of William and Margaret Johnson, Aug. 9, 1716.[34]
B. Owen, son of Arthur and Rachel Johnson, Aug. 27, 1716.
B. Christopher, son of William and Margaret Johnson, May 1, 1718.
B. Christopher, son of William and Margaret Johnson, Sept. 30, 1717.
D. Robert Johnson, May 21, 1718.
B. William, son of George and Jane Johnson, July 13, 1718.
B. Rachel Johnson's child, Oct. 14, 1720.
D. Rachel Johnson, Oct. 24, 1720.
D. Margaret Johnson, Dec. 25, 1720.
D. Daniel Johnson, Jan. 1, 1720/1.
B. Mary, dau. of George and Jane Johnson, Jan. 30, 1720/1.
B. Alexander, son of George and Jane Johnson, Apr. 5, 1723.
Bapt. Sarah, dau. of Margaret Johnson, 9th of Apr. 1725.
M. Patrick Johnson and Seely Duncan, Nov. 17, 1724.
D. Margaret Johnson, Jan. 6, 1725/6.
B. Charles, son of William and Mary Johnson, Feb. 21, 1725/6.
M. Margaret Johnson and Thomas Lacy, Apr. 30, 1726.
M. Patrick Johnson and Elinor Chambers, May 14, 1726.
D. George Johnson, Oct. 26, 1726.
D. Thomas Johnson, Oct. 26, 1727.
M. Elizabeth Johnson and Richard Lee, Jan. 26, 1727/8.
M. Jacob Johnson and Eleanor Delander, Dec. 10, 1728.

M. Jane Johnson and Alexander Rigby, Dec. 28, 1729.
M. John Johnson and Frances Powell, Nov. 18, 1731.
B. William, son of John and Frances Johnson, Aug. 16, 1732.
B. Elizabeth, dau. of Jacob and Eleanor Johnson, Apr. 16, 1733.
B. John, son of John and Frances Johnson, May 20, 1734.
M. George Johnson and Anne Cheesman, Jan. 9, 1734/5.
B. Mary, dau. of John and Frances Johnson, Dec. 7, 1735.
D. Mary Johnson, Dec. 17, 1735.
B. George, son of George and Anne Johnson, Dec. 25, 1735.
B. George, son of George and Anne Johnson, Aug. 12, 1736.
B. David, son of Sarah Johnson, Jan. 18, 1737/8.
B. Mary, dau. of John and Frances Johnson, Mar. 7, 1737/8.
B. Lettice, dau. of John and Frances Johnson, Apr. 6, 1738.
B. Jane, dau. of Jacob and Eleanor Johnson, Aug. 14, 1738.
B. Jacob, son of Jacob and Eleanor Johnson, Apr. 3, 1741.
B. John, son of John and Frances Johnson, Dec. 5, 1742.
B. William, son of George and Anne Johnson, Jan. 21, 1742/3.
B. Mildred, dau. of Jacob and Eleanor Johnson, Sept. 29, 1743.
M. William Johnson and Mary Sebastian, Jan. 5, 1743/4 (1742/3?)
M. Janet Johnson and Thomas Williams, Nov. 13, 1744.
B. John, son of William and Mary Johnson, Mar. 24, 1743/4.
B. Jane, dau. of William and Mary Johnson, June 1, 1746.
M. Jacob Johnson and Margaret Regan, Oct. 13, 1748.
M. Sarah Johnson and Henry Smith, jun: Mar. 19, 1756 (?).
B. William, son of William and Mary Johnson, June 16, 1752.
M. Jane Johnson and William Thomas, Dec. 25, 1752.
M. Lettice Johnson and Maxfield Whiting, Feb. 3, 1753.
B. Benjamin, son of Jacob and Margaret Johnson, Apr. 3, 1755.
B. Sukey, dau. of William Johnson, Feb. 2, 1757.
B. Margaret, dau. of William and Mary Johnson, Jan. 10, 1757.
B. William Sebastian, son of William and Mary Johnson, Apr. 22, 1758.
B. Charles, son of Jacob and Margaret Johnson, Nov. 25, 1759.
M. William Johnson and Winifred Gray, Feb. 24, 1760.
B. William, son of William and Winifred Johnson, Oct. 15, 1760.
M. Mary Johnson and James Jackson, Sept. 3, 1761.
M. William Johnson and Frances Goff, Nov. 20, 1762.
B. Anne, dau. of William and Frances Johnson, Feb. 6, 1764.
B. Behethland, dau. of William and Frances Johnson, Apr. 19, 1766.
B. Reuben, son of John and Jane Johnson, Jan. 17, 1767.
B. Mary, dau. of Jacob and Sarah Johnson, Apr. 29, 1767.
B. Frances, dau. of John and Mary Johnson, Nov. 30, 1767.
M. Amelia Johnson and John Keith, Jan. 5, 1768.
B. Mary Goff, dau. of William and Frances Johnson, Feb. 11, 1769.
B. George, son of Jacob and Sarah Johnson, Apr. 26, 1769.
B. Benjamin, son of Jacob and Sarah Johnson, Dec. 25, 1771.
M. Frances Johnson and John Christie, Jan. 20, 1771.
B. Margaret, dau. of John and Mary Johnson, Feb. 21, 1771.
B. William, son of John and Mary Johnson, July 2, 1772.
B. Sarah, dau. of Jacob and Sarah Johnson, Aug. 23, 1772.
M. John Johnson and Frances Dounton, July 30, 1778.
M. William Johnson and Patty Wharton, Aug. 5, 1778.
M. Anne Johnson and Jacob Smith, Nov. 1, 1781.
M. Mary Johnson and William Bennett, Nov. 9, 1782.
M. Samuel Johnson and Peggy Birch, July 28, 1785.
M. Behethland Johnson and William Mitchell, Sept. 4, 1787.
M. Sarah Jones and Richard Carver, Jan. 21, 1722/3.

B. Charles, son of Henry and Anne Jones, Sept. 14, 1725.[35]
D. John Jones, Jan. 19, 1725/6.
B. Frances, dau. of Mary Jones, Apr. 6, 1732.
M. William Jones and Mary Baxter, July 26, 1744.
M. John Jones and Eleanor Moss, Aug. 16, 1744.
B. Thomas, son of William and Elizabeth Jones, Nov. 30, 1745.
B. Charles Calvert, son of John and Eleanor Jones, June 4, and baptized July 6, 1746.
M. Matthew Jones and Rose Cavenaugh, Sept. 21, 1746.
B. Behethland, dau. of John and Eleanor Jones, July 14 and baptized Aug. 14, 1748.
M. Anne Jones and William Lord, Oct. 12, 1748.
M. William Jones and Elizabeth Alsop, Feb. 9, 1749/50.
B. Nathaniel, son of John and Eleanor Jones, Feb. 25, 1750/1.
B. Sarah, dau. of Frances Jones, Mar. 7, 1752.
M. William Jones and Jane Reiney, Apr. 20, 1752.
M. Frances Jones and Robert Rose, June 7, 1752.
B. Charles, son of John and Sarah Jones, Feb. 24, 1753.
B. Mary, dau. of William and Elizabeth Jones, May 20, 1753.
B. Sabra, dau. of John and Eleanor Jones, Oct. 7 and baptized Dec. 9, 1753.
M. Mary Jones and Thomas Fletcher, Dec. 28, 1753.
B. Anne, dau. of William and Elizabeth Jones, Feb. 21, 1755.
B. John, son of Jane Jones, Mar. 28, 1756.
B. Sukey, dau. of John and Alinda Jones, Mar. 25, 1757.
B. Henry, son of Henry and Honor Jones, June 7, 1757.
B. Charles Buirn, son of Frances Jones, Feb. 3, 1759.
M. Elizabeth Jones and David Parsons, Feb. 25, 1759.
B. Jane, dau. of John and Eleanor Jones, Mar. 16, 1762.
M. David Jones, and Mary Boswell, Feb. 18, 1763.
B. Benjamin, son of David and Anne Jones, Apr. 18, 1766.
M. Behethland Jones and John Peed, Feb. 14, 1770.
M. Joseph Jones and Mary Jordan, of King George county, Aug. 16, 1774.
M. Eleanor Jones and Daniel Hammit, Dec. 22, 1774.
M. Sabra Jones and William Crank, Feb. 8, 1778.
M. Jane Jones and Samuel Marshall, June 13, 1782.
M. James Jones and Mary Wilkerson, Apr. 6, 1786.
M. Susanna Jones and John Price, May 5, 1786.
M. Nancy Jones and Richard Allen, Feb. 4, 1788.
M. Mildred Jones and John Whiting, Dec. 26, 1788.
B. Winifred, dau. of Elizabeth Jordan, Oct. 4, 1745.
M. Elizabeth Jordan and William Ward, Dec. 25, 1753.
M. Alexander Jordan and Behethland Gravat, Oct. 30, 1758.
M. Esther Jordan and William Derrick, Dec. 20, 1762.
M. Mary Jordan of King George county and Joseph Jones, Aug. 16, 1774.
D. William Joy, husband of Anne Joy, Jan. 18, 1717/18.
B. William, son of Martha Joy, Dec. 15, 1737.
B. Isaac, son of Martha Joy, Dec. 30, 1743.
M. Anne Joy and Joseph Goss, Dec. 24, 1747.
B. Anne, dau. of Martha Joy, Apr. 5, 1748.
B. Mary, dau. of Martha Joy, Feb. 19, 1750/1.
M. Anne Joy and Patrick Sherman, Aug. 9, 1768.
M. Isaac Joy and Elizabeth McCant, Mar. 23, 1770.
B. William, son of Isaac and Elizabeth Joy, Jan. 26, 1771.
M. Elizabeth Joy, and Henry Goss, Aug. 8, 1773.

K

B. Elizabeth, dau. of John and Elizabeth Keith, Nov. 4, 1759.
B. Jane, dau. of John and Elizabeth Keith, July 2, 1764.
M. John Keith and Amelia Johnson, Jan. 5, 1768.
M. Amie Keith and Peter Puckett, Dec. 27, 1775.
D. Lionel Kelly, Aug. 10, 1717.
B. Elizabeth, dau. of Philip and Sarah Kelly, Dec. 6, 1715.
D. Sarah Kelly, Oct. 8, 1718.
B. Sarah, dau. of Wilford and Jane Kelly, Nov. 10, 1721.
M. John Kelly and Jane Moss, Dec. 21, 1722.
B. Elizabeth, dau. of John and Jane Kelly, --1723.
B. James, son of Alexander and Diana Kelly, Nov. 30, 1725.
M. John Kelly and Mary Laton, Dec. 4, 1725.
B. Alse, dau. of John and Mary Kelly, Oct. 20, 1726.
M. Frances Kelly and Sylvester Moss, July 7, 1727.
B. Behethland, dau. of John and Mary Kelly, Mar. 30, 1728.
M. Mary Kelly and William Francomb, June 22, 1728.
B. Thomas, son of Wilford and Jane Kelly, --1728.
D. Wilford Kelly, Aug. 24, 1728.
D. John Kelly, Dec. 16, 1730.
B. Frances, dau. of John and Mary Kelly, Apr. 10, 1731.
B. Anthony Buckner, son of Jane Kelly alias Thomas, Apr. 30, 1731.
M. William Kelly and Margaret Dew, Apr. 24, 1732.
M. Jane Kelly and Henry Smith, Sept. 24, 1733.
M. Edmund Kelly and Jane Gregg, June 15, 1736.[36]
B. Katherine, dau. of Edmund and Jane Kelly, Mar. 4, 1736/7.
M. Sarah Kelly and Thomas Glover, Sept. 1, 1737.
B. William, son of Mary Kelly, Jan. 2, 1737/8.
M. Maria Kelly and William Goff, Sept. 8, 1738.
B. John, son of Edmund and Jane Kelly, Apr. 11, 1739.
B. Vinson, son of Edmund and Jane Kelly, Aug. 8, 1741.
M. Samuel Kelly and Behethland White, Aug. 25, 1741.
B. Wilford, son of Samuel and Behethland Kelly, June 23, 1742.
M. Jane Kelly and Samuel Whiting, Aug. 29, 1744.
B. Tabitha, dau. of Samuel and Behethland Kelly, Nov. 7, 1744.
M. Elizabeth Kelly and Michael Hall, Dec. 29, 1744.
B. William, son of Thomas and Anne Kelly, Apr. 11, 1745.
B. Charles, son of Margaret Kelly, Apr. 30, 1746.
M. Elizabeth Kelly and Richard Dane, June 30, 1746.
M. Mary Kelly and William Lacy, Dec. 4, 1746.
B. Sarah, dau. of Samuel and Behethland Kelly, Dec. 27, 1746.
B. Jasper, son of Thomas and Anne Kelly, Feb. 21, 1746/7.
B. Edmund, son of Samuel and Behethland Kelly, Sept. 11, 1748.[37]
M. William Kelly and Phillis McIntosh, Aug. 22, 1751.
M. Behethland Kelly and John Gravat, Dec. 27, 1751.
M. Mary Kelly and James Hartley, Aug. 25, 1754.
B. Mary, dau. of William and Phillis Kelly, Apr. 21, 1755.
M. James Kelly and Eleanor Burnsplat, Apr. 15, 1757.
M. William Kelly and Jane Minor, Mar. 30, 1758.
B. Isaac, son of William and Phillis Kelly, Aug. 15, 1760.
M. Tabitha Kelly and Patrick Clark, Aug. 13, 1764.
M. Vincent Kelly and Elizabeth Sharpe, Jan. 26, 1769.
M. Woodford Kelly and Mildred Tunnell, Feb. 4, 1769.
M. Winifred Kelly and Thomas Bateman, Feb. 7, 1771.
M. Thomas Kelton and Margaret Berry, Dec. 24, 1726.

M. John Kendall of Washington Parish and Frances Sharpe of this Parish, Sept. 22, 1737.
B. Thomas, son of John and Frances Kendall, Dec. 1, 1738.
M. John Kendall and Elizabeth Frank of Washington Parish, Apr. 24, 1746.
B. Molly, dau. of George and Margaret Kendall, May 2, 1757.
M. Hugh Kennedy and Mildred Hutcheson, Nov. 6, 1735.
M. John Kennedy and Rose Sudduth, June 21, 1736.
B. Mildred, dau. of Hugh and Mildred Kennedy, May 22, 1736.
B. Isaac, son of William and Margaret Kennedy, June 12, 1758.
M. Thomas Kennedy and Frances Lucas, Oct. 9, 1763.
M. Behethland Kennedy and Luke Hughes, July 10, 1779.
M. Martha Kenneman and John Sutton, Sept. 17, 1723.
M. Joanna Kennet (Kemmet?) and Joseph Lane, May 22, 1754.
M. Michael Kenny and Margaret Bignell, July 29, 1750.
M. Peter Kerr and Sarah Stribling, Aug. 23, 1728.[38]
M. Sarah Kerr and Charles Martin, Oct. 1, 1736.
B. John, son of Jeremiah and Anne Kersey, Mar. 20, 1758.
M. Robert Key and Elizabeth Strother, Dec. 13, 1762.
M. Mary Key and Enoch Strother, Feb. 12, 1763.
D. John Kidwell, June 16, 1725.
M. Elizabeth Kidwell and William Bowling, Sept. 7, 1726.
M. Mary Kidwell and Samuel Thornsberry, Apr. 20, 1744.
M. Peter Kilgore and Mary Haydon, Nov. 1, 1722.
D. William King, Dec. 21, 1726.
M. Robert King and Margaret Sebastian, Apr. 26, 1727.
D. Joseph King, Sr., Sept. 26, 1728.
M. Samuel King and Jane Flagg, Nov. 11, 1729.
B. Joshua, son of Robert and Margaret King, Jan. 3, 1730/1.
B. Josepha, son of Joseph and Sarah King, Feb. 21, 1731/2.
B. Sarah, dau. of Samuel and Jane King, Mar. 29, 1732.
M. Joseph King and Sarah Carrico, May 7, 1731.
B. Anne, dau. of Robert and Margaret King, July 16, 1733.
B. Jane, dau. of Samuel and Jane King, Aug. 12, 1733.
B. Joel, son of Joseph and Sarah King, May 10, 1734.
M. William King and Mary Trigger, Aug. 2, 1735.
B. William, son of Robert and Margaret King, May 29, 1736.
B. Nimrod, son of William and Mary King, Oct. 29, 1736.
B. Susanna, dau. of Joseph and Sarah King, Dec. 18, 1736.
B. Robert, son of Robert and Mary King, Apr. 18, 1739.
B. Mary, dau. of Joseph and Sarah King, May 2, 1739.
B. Benjamin, son of Robert and Mary King, Nov. 19, 1741.
B. Isaac, son of Robert and Mary King, Nov. 17, 1745.
M. Thomas King and Jane Thomas, May 19, 1771.
B. William, son of Richard and Jane King, June 12, 1772.
M. Sarah Kirk and William Bowling, June 24, 1726.
M. Hezekiah Kirk and Behethland Bennett, Feb. 10, 1778.
M. Jeremiah Kirk and Anne Monroe, Aug. 18, 1785.
D. Thomas Kitchen, Mar. 20, 1715/16.
M. Anthony Kitchen and Mary Overall, Aug. 31, 1727.
B. Sarah, dau. of Anthony and Mary (Kitchen?) --1729.
B. William, son of Anthony and Mary Kitchen, Feb. 23, 1731/2.
B. Mary, dau. of Anthony and Mary Kitchen, Nov. 14, 1734.
B. Anthony, son of Anthony (and Mary?) Kitchen, Aug. 22, 1736.
B. Jane, dau. of Anthony Kitchen, Jan. 26, 1738/9.
B. George, son of Anthony and Mary Kitchen, May 16, 1741.
B. Elizabeth, dau. of Anthony and Mary Kitchen, Aug. 20, 1743.

B. Anthony, son of Sarah Kitchen, Nov. 7, 1745.
M. Sarah Kitchen and Caesar Franklin, Aug. 28, 1746.
B. Peggy, dau. of Anthony and Mary Kitchen, June 28, 1747.
D. Anthony Kitchen, Mar. 17, 1746/7.
M. Mary Kitchen and John Lee Wright, Aug. 8, 1751.
M. Elizabeth Kitchen and Joseph Lacy, Sept. 10, 1759.
B. James, son of Thomas and Mary Kitchen, Oct. 4, 1756.
B. William, son of Thomas and Elizabeth Kitchen, Oct. 14, 1756.
B. Thomas, son of Anthony and Sarah Kitchen, Jan. 4, 1769.
B. Sukey, dau. of Anthony and Sarah Kitchen, Mar. 1, 1763.
B. George Monroe, son of Anthony (and Sarah?) Kitchen, Feb. 7, 1766.
B. Sarah, dau. of Anthony and Sarah Kitchen, Dec. 11, 1770.
B. Jane, dau. of Anthony and Sarah Kitchen, June 4, 1772.
D. William Knight, son of Catherine Moss, Apr. 2, 1716.[39]
M. William Knight and Jane Butler, Dec. 26, 1734.
M. Jane Knight and John Demsoe, July 6, 1737.
M. Mary Knight and Thomas Fletcher, Mar. 2, 1742/3.
M. Lewis Knowland and Mary Griggs, Mar. 26, 1771.
M. John Knowling and Mildred Stribling, Apr. 11, 1776.

L

M. John Lackey and Sarah Payne, June 6, 1737.
M. Thomas Lacy and Judith Rawlings, Nov. 9, 1716.
B. John, son of Thomas and Judith Lacy, Oct. 30, 1717.
B. Anne, dau. of Thomas and Judith Lacy, Jan. 28, 1720/1.
B. Thomas, son of Thomas and Judith Lacy, Feb. 19, 1723/4.
D. Lucia (?Judith) Lacy, Nov. 11, 1725.
M. Thomas Lacy and Margaret Johnson, Apr. 30, 1726.
B. William, son of Thomas and Sarah Lacy, Dec. 5, 1725.
B. Sarah, dau. of Thomas and Margaret Lacy, May 6, 1731.
B. Jacob, son of Thomas and Margaret Lacy, Jan. 2, 1733/4.
B. Joseph, son of Thomas and Margaret Lacy, Jan. 25, 1736/7.
D. John, son of Thomas Lacy, Dec. 5, 1739.
M. William Lacy and Mary Kelly, Dec. 4, 1746.
B. Anne, dau. of William and Mary Lacy, Apr. 16, 1747.[40]
B. John, son of William and Sarah (?Mary) Lacy, Sept. 3, 1748.
M. Margaret Lacy and Mason French, Apr. 16, 1749.
M. Mary Lacy and Thomas Parcmane, Aug. 28, 1751.
M. Joseph Lacy and Elizabeth Kitchen, Sept. 10, 1759.
B. Thomas, son of Joseph and Elizabeth Lacy, Jan. 1, 1764.
M. Anne Lambert and John Wilson, Oct. 28, 1759.
B. Mary, dau. of William and Sarah Lampton, June 30, 1734.
B. William, son of John and Catherine Land, Apr. 9, 1771.
B. Elisha, son of Elizabeth Land, Nov. 28, 1772.
D. James Landon, Mar. 21, 1731/2.
M. Joseph Lane and Joanna Kenneth (Kemmet?), May 22, 1754.
M. Mary Latham and Benjamin Bowling, July 27, 1725.
B. Sarah, dau. of John and Mary Latham, Feb. 21, 1725/6.
B. Franklin, son of John and Mary Latham, Mar. 26, 1728.
B. Alse, dau. of John and Mary (Latham?) --1729.
B. Shadwell, son of John and Mary Latham, Jan. 24, 1730/1.
B. Hannah, dau. of Stephen and Joanna Latham, Apr. 19, 1739.
M. Mary Laton and John Kelly, Dec. 4, 1725.
D. Henry Lavine (Savine?), June 5, 1725.
D. Sophia Lawyer (Sawyer?) Mar. 13, 1733/4.

D. John Lawyer (Sawyer?), Mar. 19, 1733/4.
D. Edward Lawyer (Layer), Jan. 17, 1739/40.[41]
M. Richard Lee and Margaret Brady, July 8, 1723.
M. Richard Lee and Elizabeth Johnson, Jan. 26, 1727/8.
D. Richard Lee, Senr: Apr. 4, 1731.
B. Mildred, dau. of Richard and Elizabeth Lee, Aug. 2, 1731.
M. Lettice Lee and John Corbin, Sept. 1, 1737.
B. Anne, dau. of Richard and Elizabeth Lee, Apr. 2, 1738.
D. Margaret, widow of Richard Lee, Feb. 9, 1739/40 (1740/1?).
B. Bennett, son of John and Sarah Lee, Feb. 24, 1739/40.
B. Sarah, dau. of Richard and Elizabeth Lee, Dec. 30, 1741.
D. Elizabeth Lee, July 4, 1743.
M. Richard Lee and Mary Rose, June 29, 1744.
B. William, son of John and Sarah Lee, Oct. 20, 1744.
M. Margaret Lee and James Floyd, Feb. 20, 1749/50.
M. John Lee and Fanny Underwood, Mar. 2, 1790.
M. Joseph Lee and Sarah Fewel, July 22, 1792.
M. Sarah Leach and Henry Smith, Dec. 29, 1767.
B. Elisha, son of Thomas and Rosamond Leftwich, June 28, 1738.
B. Mary, dau. of Elisha and Priscilla Leftwich, Sept. 2, 1742.
B. Anne, dau. of Elisha and Priscilla Leftwich, Oct. 22, 1744.
B. Susanna, dau. of Elisha and Priscilla Leftwich, Oct. 6, 1746.
B. Rosamond, dau. of Elisha and Priscilla Leftwich, Aug. 22, 1748.
M. Elizabeth Legg and Rehobeth Barnfather, Dec. 31, 1724.
D. John Lenpey, Dec. 18, 1717.
D. Mary Leonard, Dec. 29, 1717.
M. Hannah Leonard and William Heselton, July 7, 1765.
B. Alice, dau. of Abraham and Anne Levee (Levy?), Sept. 28, 1748.
B. Jacob, son of Abraham and Anne Levee, Oct. 23, 1759.
B. John, son of Frances Levee, Feb. 25, 1773.
M. Sarah Levy and William Trigger, Feb. 1, 1786.
M. Mary Lewis and James Power, Oct. 19, 1724.
M. Thomas Lewis and Elizabeth Mealy, Oct. 5, 1730.
B. Daniel, son of Thomas and Elizabeth Lewis, Oct. 14, 1733.
M. Benjamin Lewis and Sarah Handley, Aug. 31, 1734.
D. Benjamin Lewis, Sept. 2, 1735.
M. Sarah Lewis and Leonard Martin, Nov. 27, 1736.
M. Elizabeth Lewis and William Lord, Oct. 23, 1738.
M. Daniel Lewis and Elizabeth Rose, Aug. 31, 1762.
B. Thomas, son of Daniel and Elizabeth Lewis, Apr. 2, 1764.
B. Benjamin, son of Benjamin and Elizabeth Lewis, Apr. 17, 1769.
M. Elizabeth Lewis and Benoni Stratton, Sept. 29, 1772.
M. Clarinda Lewis and Isaac Rogers, Dec. 11, 1791.
M. John Limit and Anne Bateman, Apr. 6, 1751.
B. Elizabeth, dau. of John and Anne Limit, Sept. 10, 1753.
B. George, son of John and Anne Limit, July 16, 1755.
M. Elizabeth Limit and James Buchanan, Dec. 7, 1777.
B. Anne, dau. of Dennis and Barbara Lindsay, Oct. 14, 1725.
B. Moses, son of Dennis and Barbara Lindsay, Jan. 31, 1727/8.
M. Margaret Lindsay and John Haynes, Sept. 8, 1728.
B. Anne, dau. of Dennis and Barbara Lindsay, Jan. 20, 1730/1.
B. Wilkeson, dau. of Dennis and Barbara Lindsay, July 20, 1733.
B. Sarah, dau. of Dennis and Barbara Lindsay, Feb. 20, 1735/6.
B. Dennis, son of Dennis and Barbara Lindsay, May 8, 1738.
M. John Lindsay and Sarah Clift, Jan. 3, 1739/40.
M. Barbara Lindsay and Josias Branham, Aug. 5, 1742.

B. Winifred, dau. of Matthew and Anne Lindsay, Apr. 14, 1746.
M. Robert Lindsley and Anne McLeod, Aug. 21, 1744.
M. Ambrose Lipscomb and Winifred Mardus, Dec. 23, 1785.
M. Anne Lloyd and John Hyatt, Jan. 7, 1717/18.
M. Sarah Lloyd and William Dick, July 25, 1732.
D. Benjamin Lloyd, Jan. 15, 1736/7.
M. Henry Locke and Sarah Dreem, Sept. 17, 1722.
M. Henry Locke and Elizabeth Blakeman, Feb. 6, 1724/5.[42]
M. William Long and Eleanor Bolton, May 15, 1749.
B. Sarah, dau. of William and Anne Long, May 2, 1753.
B. Elizabeth, dau. of William and Anne Long, Feb. 18, 1756.
B. Anne, dau. of William and Anne Long, Apr. 8, 1758.
B. David, son of William and Anne Long, July 5, 1760.
B. Mary, dau. of William and Anne Long, July 8, 1762.
M. Elizabeth Long and John Tunnell, Feb. 13, 1774.
M. William Long and Joanna Sacheverel (Chivrel?), Dec. 30, 1790.
M. William Lord and Elizabeth Lewis, Oct. 23, 1738.
B. William, son of William and Elizabeth Lord, Jan. 12, 1738/9.
D. Elizabeth Lord, Sept. 3, 1741.
M. William Lord and Clary Mannard, Jan. 8, 1741/2.
B. Robert, son of William and Clary Lord, Oct. 5, 1747.
M. William Lord and Anne Jones, Oct. 12, 1748.
B. William, son of William and Anne Lord, Apr. 9, 1756.
M. William Lord and Frances Stratton, Oct. 31, 1756.
B. Benjamin, son of William and Frances Lord, Mar. 15, 1757.
B. Clary, dau. of William and Anne (Frances?) Lord, Jan. 12, 1762.
B. Elisha, son of William and Frances Lord, Aug. 10, 1766.
B. Lucy, dau. of William and Frances Lord, Jan. 10, 1769.
B. Frances, dau. of William and Frances Lord, Feb. 15, 1771.
B. Willoughby, son of William and Frances Lord, May 7, 1772.
M. William Lord and Nelly Wilson, Apr. 7, 1780.
D. William Lowell, Oct. 23, 1725.
B. Katherine, dau. of Hannah Lowell (Sowell?), Feb. 2, 1726/7.
M. John Lowry and Elizabeth Seaton, Apr. 23, 1726.
D. Elizabeth Lowry, Mar. 25, 1733.
M. Sarah Lowry and Moses Hubbard, Mar. 23, 1726/7.
B. Elizabeth, dau. of Thomas and Elizabeth Lowther, Apr. 15, 1728.
M. Anthony Lucas and Sarah Stransford, Nov. 4, 1737.
B. Anne, dau. of Anthony and Sarah Lucas, Jan. 7, 1737/8.
B. Augustine, son of Anthony and Sarah Lucas, Sept. 6, 1743.
B. Frances Lucas, Jan. 2, 1743/4. (?died)
B. Annenah, dau. of Frances Lucas, Apr. 2, 1747.
M. Anne Lucas and Thomas Evans, Feb. 4, 1753.
B. Anne, dau. of Sarah Lucas, Nov. 16, 1753.
M. Frances Lucas and Thomas Kennedy, Oct. 9, 1763.
B. Mark, son of Sarah Lucas, Aug. 5, 1764.
B. Anthony, son of Francis Lucas, June 6, 1772.
B. Susanna, dau. of Sarah Lucas, Mar. 13, 1774.
B. Henry, son of Sarah Lucas, Aug. 3, 1784.
D. Mrs. Frances Lund, dau. of Capt. Samuel Lund, dec'd., Oct. 19, 1716.
M. Elizabeth Lund and Townshend Washington, Dec. 22, 1726.
M. Timothy Lyons (Lines?) and Sarah Sebastian, Jan. 11, 1746/7.
M. Jane McCant and Thomas Carrico, Oct. 4, 1744.
M. James McCant and Elizabeth Walker, Mar. 15, 1747/8.
B. Elizabeth, dau. of James and Elizabeth McCant, Dec. 27, 1748.
B. Joseph, son of James and Elizabeth McCant, Oct. 15, 1751.

B. James, son of James and Elizabeth McCant, Dec. 17, 1753.
B. Sally, dau. of James and Elizabeth McCant, Aug. 17, 1757.
B. James, son of James and Elizabeth McCant, Sept. 22, 1762.
M. Elizabeth McCant and Isaac Joy, Mar. 23, 1770.
B. Dorothy, dau. of Margaret McCarty, July 8, 1724.
D. Robert McCarty, Jan. 27, 1725/6.
M. Winifred McCarty of Overwharton Parish and Robert Massey, Dec. 20, 1728.
M. Thomas McCarty and Griselle Matthews, Dec. 23, 1728.
M. Hugh McCarty and Elinor Sullivan, Apr. 22, 1730.
D. Mrs. Anne McCarty, Jan. 12, 1731/2.[43]
B. William, son of Mary McCarty, Feb. 3, 1733/4.
B. Katherine, dau. of Margaret McCarty, Mar. 19, 1735/6.
M. Margaret McCarty and Henry Bussey, July 11, 1741.
M. Catherine McCarty and George Gravat, May 9, 1756.
M. Daniel McCarty and Mary Mercer, Apr. 3, 1764.
M. Daniel McCarty and Winifred Thornton, Jan. 15, 1765.
B. James, son of Anne McCleaning, Mar. 12, 1732/3.
M. John McCormick and Elizabeth Suttle of Hanover Parish, Mar. 8, 1735/6.
M. Rev. Roderick McColluck and Elizabeth Weedon of Washington Parish, Feb. 17, 1734/5.
D. James McCulloh, Dec. 12, 1735.
B. Winifred, dau. of James and Anne McDaniel, Apr. 2, 1748.
M. James McDonald and Martha Carruthers of Overwharton Parish, Nov. 15, 1731.
M. Edward McDonald and Elizabeth Smith, Feb. 6, 1735/6.
M. Mary McDonald and John Alsop, Aug. 20, 1737.
M. Alinda McDonald and Benjamin Wilson, Feb. 27, 1757.
B. Jane and Margaret, daus. of Briant and Judith McDonald, Jan. 30, 1760.
M. William McDonald and Ursula Gravat, July 1, 1767.
M. Jane McDonald and David Briggs, June 1, 1771.
M. James McDuff and Mary Walker, Mar. 3, 1757.
M. Anne McFarland and William Scipier, Feb. 17, 1750/1.
D. Mr. Daniel McGill, Nov. 5, 1725.
D. Sarah McGill, Gentlewoman, Nov. 1749.
B. Mary, dau. of John and Margaret McGilvray, Sept. 14, 1739.
M. Malcolm McIntosh and Mary Wood, Nov. 24, 1743.
B. Peggie, dau. of James and Phillis McIntosh, Nov. 10, 1748.
B. James, son of James McIntosh, Jan. 30, 1750/1.
M. Mary McIntosh and Clement Sacheverel, Aug. 11, 1751.
M. Phillis McIntosh and William Kelly, Aug. 22, 1751.
M. James McIntosh and Sarah Howell, Dec. 17, 1773.
B. Elizabeth, dau. of James and Sarah McKay, Nov. 5, 1720.
D. Sarah McKay, Nov. 15, 1720.
D. Elizabeth, dau. of James and Sarah McKay, dec'd., Jan. 25, 1720/1.
D. James McKay, Apr. 17, 1733.
B. Sarah, dau. of John and Margaret McKee, Apr. 23, 1738.
M. The Reverend Mr. William McKay, Rector of Hanover Parish, and Barbara Fitzhugh of this Parish, Feb. 6, 1738/9.
B. Thomas, son of Margaret McKee, Mar. 4, 1764.
B. Mary, dau. of Margaret McKee, Aug. 10, 1767.
M. Anne McKey and Thomas Emerson, Apr. 17, 1743.
B. Margaret, dau. of Anne McKinny (?), Mar. 15, 1753.
M. Richard McLachlan and Elizabeth Smith, Jan. 31, 1760.
B. Jane, dau. of Richard and Elizabeth McLachlan, Oct. 9, 1762.
M. John McLean and Eleanor Bell, Apr. 14, 1745.
M. Mary McLean and John Whiting, Aug. 10, 1791.

M. Anne McLeod and Robert Lindsley, Aug. 21, 1744.
M. Elizabeth Mahoney and John Hill, Oct. 1, 1716.
M. John MacClanin and Elizabeth Barker, Mar. 24, 1793.
M. Sarah Mackall and Samuel Sims, July 10, 1735.
M. Mary Maddox and John Curly, May 9, 1767.
B. Mary, dau. of Dennis and Mary Mahony, Apr. 29, 1725.
B. Dennis, son of Dennis and Rebecca Mahony, Mar. 29, 1728.
B. William, son of Dennis and Rebecca Mahony, Mar. 15, 1731/2.
B. Elizabeth, dau. of Dennis and Rebecca Mahony, Aug. 20, 1736.
B. Benjamin, son of Dennis and Rebecca Mahony, Jan. 24, 1738/9.
D. Dennis Mahony, Sept. 23, 1740.
B. John, son of Dennis (dec'd.?) and Rebecca Mahony, May 26, 1741.
D. Sarah Mahony, Nov. 22, 1744.
M. William Mahony and Rebecca Oliver, Sept. 15, 1759.
M. Henry Duval Manjeur and Leila Drummond, Apr. 30, 1758.
B. Henry Duval, son of Henry Duval and Leila Manjeur, Jan. 31, 1759.
M. Robert Mannard and Clary Derrick, May 27, 1723.[44]
D. Elizabeth, dau. of Robert and Clary Mannard, Sept. 6, 1724.
B. Clary, dau. of Robert and Clary Mannard, July 12, 1726.
B. William, son of Robert and Clary Mannard, Apr. 15, 1732.
B. John and Robert, sons of Robert and Clary Mannard, Nov. 6, 1734.
B. Derrick, son of Robert and Clary Mannard, Nov. 1, 1737.
M. Clary Mannard and William Lord, Jan. 8, 1741/2.
M. William Mannard and Martha Davis, Aug. 13, 1752.
M. Keziah Mannard and Benjamin Truslow, Mar. 12, 1786.
M. Clary Mannard and William Richardson, Jan. 16, 1791.
M. Amie Mannard and Aaron Owens, May 13, 1791.
M. Elizabeth Mardus and Joseph Rawlings, May 25, 1778.
M. Aaron Mardus and Mary Thomas, Mar. 12, 1785.
M. Winifred Mardus and Ambrose Lipscomb, Dec. 23, 1785.
M. Elizabeth Mardus and Robert Alsop, Jan. 3, 1791.
M. Moses Mardus and Mary Price, Feb. 27, 1791.
M. Elizabeth Mardus and Bartlett White, Mar. 2, 1792.
M. John Markous and Mary Anne Grigsby, Sept. 1, 1763.
B. Anne, dau. of John and Elizabeth Marshall, Apr. 29, 1726.
D. Anne, widow of Thomas Marshall, Mar. 28, 1740.
M. Rush Marshall and Joanna Peed, Nov. 23, 1779.
M. Samuel Marshall and Jane Jones, June 13, 1782.
M. Anne Martin and Joseph Sebastian, Feb. 6, 1717/8.
B. Rose, dau. of Leonard and Sarah Martin, Nov. 3, 1718.
B. Anne, dau. of Leonard and Sarah Martin, June 3, 1722.
B. John, son of Leonard and Sarah Martin, ...1724/5.
B. Leonard, son of Leonard and Sarah Martin, July 14, 1726.
M. Charles Martin and Sarah Kerr, Oct. 1, 1736.
M. Leonard Martin and Sarah Lewis, Nov. 27, 1736.
B. Anne, dau. of Leonard and Sarah Martin, Aug. 24, 1738.
M. John Martin and Lucy Todd, Nov. 5, 1742.
D. John Martin, Nov. 24, 1742.
B. Leonard, son of Leonard and Sarah Martin, Mar. 17, 1742/3.
B. James, son of Lucy Martin, May 22, 1744.
B. Sarah, dau. of Leonard and Sarah Martin, July 10, 1746.
M. Sarah Martin and Alexander Douglas, Sept. 8, 1751.
M. Anne Martin and Thomas Mustin, Jan. 19, 1759.
M. Sarah Martin and John Tunnell, Feb. 18, 1763.
M. Leonard Martin and Elizabeth More, Dec. 28, 1764.
B. William, son of Leonard and Mary Martin, Dec. 31, 1772.

M. Elizabeth Mason and John Bushell, June 26, 1748.
M. Nehemiah Rodham Mason and Sarah Dade, Feb. 12, 1762.
B. John Blackston, son of N. R. B. Mason, Mar. 10, 1769.
M. George Mason and Elizabeth Hooe, Apr. 22, 1784.
M. William Mason and Anne Stuart, July 11, 1793.
B. Anne, dau. of Dade and Elizabeth Massey, Mar. 19, 1719/20.
D. Benjamin Massey, June 24, 1725.
M. Elizabeth Massey and Henry Dade, July 7, 1726.
M. Elizabeth Massey and James Reddish, Aug. 19, 1726.
M. Robert Massey and Winifred McCarty of Overwharton Parish, Dec. 20, 1728.
B. Betty, dau. of Robert and Winifred Massey, Sept. 8, 1731.
M. Dade Massey and Parthenia Alexander, Jan. 17, 1731/2.[45]
B. Lee, son of Dade and Parthenia Massey, Sept. 19, 1732.
B. Robert, son of Robert and Winifred Massey, Sept. 10, 1733.
B. Dade, son of Dade and Parthenia Massey, Oct. 10, 1734.
D. Dade Massey, Jun'r: Feb. 7, 1734/5.
D. Capt. Dade Massey, Apr. 16, 1735.
B. Winifred, dau. of Robert and Winifred Massey, Sept. 6, 1735.
M. Parthenia Massey and Townshend Dade, Jun'r: May 6, 1736.
M. John Massey and Elizabeth Powell, June 12, 1736.
M. Anne Massey and Francis Wright, Dec. 7, 1737.
B. Anne, dau. of Robert and Winifred Massey, Aug. 6, 1738.
B. Frances, dau. of Robert and Winifred Massey, Sept. 22, 1740.
M. Sigismund Massey and Mary Stuart, Apr. 4, 1743.
B. Jane, dau. of Sigismund and Mary Massey, Feb. 8, 1743/4.
B. Dade, son of Thomas and Eleanor Massey, Mar. 2, 1745/6.[46]
B. Sallie, dau. of Benjamin and Elizabeth Massey, Mar. 8, 1745/6.
D. Sigismund Massey, June 16, 1746.
B. Sigismunda Mary, dau. of Sigismund (dec.?) and Mary Massey, June 28, 1746.
B. Dade, son of Benjamin and Elizabeth Massey, Jan. 6, 1747/8.
B. Taliaferro, son of Benjamin and Elizabeth Massey, Apr. 22, 1749.
M. Betty Massey and John Washington, Nov. 17, 1749.
B. Frances, dau. of Benjamin and Elizabeth Massey, July 10, 1751.
B. Thomas, son of Thomas and Elizabeth (?) Massey, June 1, 1752.
M. Behethland Massey and Thomas Bunbury, Aug. 30, 1752.
M. Mary Massey and Horatio Dade, Jan. 14, 1753.
B. Robert, son of Thomas and Eleanor Massey, Nov. 16, 1757.
B. Anne, dau. of Charles and Martha Massey, Jan. 21, 1758.
B. Mary, dau. of Thomas and Mary (Eleanor?) Massey, Apr. 15, 1760.
M. Jane Massey and John Waugh, Apr. 22, 1761.
M. Winifred Massey and Elisha Powell, Dec. 20, 1761.
B. John, son of Thomas and Eleanor Massey, Sept. 20, 1762.
B. Martha, dau. of Charles and Martha Massey, Sept. 22, 1762.
B. Eleanor, dau. of Thomas and Eleanor Massey, Mar. 24, 1765.
M. Sigismunda Mary Massey and William Alexander, Apr. 18, 1765.
B. Winifred, dau. of Charles and Martha Massey, Dec. 4, 1765.
M. Elizabeth Massey and John (?) Coad, Dec. 6, 1766.
M. Sigismund Massey and Sarah Short, July 16, 1772.
M. William Massey and Hannah Settle, Feb. 8, 1784.
M. Anne Massey and John Perry, May 26, 1785.
M. Eleanor Massey and Huse (Hughes?) Mastin, June 1, 1786.
M. Lovell Massey and Sarah Whiting, Dec. 28, 1786.
M. Eleanor Massey and John Washington, Dec. 24, 1787.
M. Elizabeth Massey and James Grant, Jan. 10, 1793.
M. Eleanor Mastin and Thomas Prestridge, Dec. 29, 1726.
M. Huse (Hughes?) Mastin and Eleanor Massey, June 1, 1786.

M. Patrick Matthews of Nanjemoy Parish and Elizabeth Evans of this Parish, Aug. 17, 1725.
M. Griselle Matthews and Thomas McCarty, Dec. 23, 1728.
M. John Matthews and Anne Bussey, July 21, 1754.
B. Daniel, son of John and Elizabeth Matthews, Apr. 4, 1755.
B. Elizabeth and Sarah, daus. of John and Elizabeth Matthews, Apr. 2, 1757.
B. Mary, dau. of John and Elizabeth Matthews, Jan. 28, 1760.
B. Mildred, dau. of John and Anne Matthews, June 23, 1761.
B. John, son of John and Elizabeth Matthews, May 5, 1768.
M. Mary Matthews and Andrew Grant, Apr. 26, 1770.
M. William Matthews and Anne Mary Grant, Dec. 5, 1781.
D. Elizabeth, dau. of Thomas and Mary May (?), Oct. 22, 1724.
D. Sarah Mealy, Sept. 27, 1718.
D. Elizabeth Mealy, June 29, 1725.
B. Mary, dau. of Daniel and Margaret Mealy, ...1723/4.
M. Elizabeth Mealy and Thomas Lewis, Oct. 5, 1730.
D. Margaret, wife of Daniel Mealy, Dec. 15, 1738.
D. Daniel Mealy, Mar. 14, 1742/3 (1741/2?).
D. John Mease, Apr. 10, 1733.
D. Mary Mease, Apr. 23, 1747.
M. James Mehorner and Elizabeth Gravat, Feb. 7, 1742/3.
B. Sarah, dau. of James and Elizabeth Mehorner, Apr. 15, 1744.
B. Dennis, son of James and Elizabeth Mehorner, Dec. 9, 1745.
B. James, son of James and Elizabeth Mehorner, Jan. 19,11748/9.
B. Benjamin, son of Dennis and Margaret Mehorner, Oct. 24, 1759.
B. Henry, son of Dennis and Margaret Mehorner, Sept. 12, 1761.
M. Dennis Mehorner and Jane Carver, Sept. 8, 1766.
B. John, son of Dennis and Margaret Mehorner, July 7, 1768.
B. Elizabeth, dau. of Dennis and Jane Mehorner, Sept. 12, 1772.
B. James, son of Dennis and Jane Mehorner, Mar. 24, 1774.
M. Benjamin Mehorner and Margaret Noling, Apr. 5, 1778.
M. Dennis Mehorner and Sarah Thompson, Feb. 21, 1781.
M. Thomas Mehorner and Bethea Evans, Mar. 30, 1786.
M. Henry Mehorner and Leah Skinner, Sept. 13, 1788.
M. Benjamin Mehorner and Elizabeth Wiggins, Oct. 24, 1790.
M. Eli Mehorner and Letty Owens, June 23, 1792.
M. Mary Mercer and Daniel McCarty, Apr. 3, 1764.
M. Elizabeth (Meredith?) and Alexander Gordon, ...1716.
M. Elizabeth Mifflin and James Cope and Hanover Parish, Dec. 17, 1746.
M. Elizabeth Miller and Jacob Williams, Dec. 3, 1747.
M. Thomas Mills and Mary Bussey, Jan. 2, 1748/9.
M. Francis Mills and Margaret Handley, Apr. 6, 1751.
B. Lizzy, dau. of Francis and Margaret Mills, Mar. 19, 1752.
M. Margaret Mills and Henry Davis, Nov. 5, 1758.
M. Hannah Mills and James Brown, Jan. 31, 1786.
M. Callehill Minnis and Elizabeth Holeman, Nov. 16, 1740.
B. Frances, dau. of Callehill and Elizabeth Minnis, Sept. 23, 1741.
B. Mary, dau. of Callehill and Elizabeth Minnis, Oct. 5, 1743.
B. Charles, son of Callehill and Elizabeth Minnis, Jan. 21, 1745/6.
B. Callehill, son of Callehill and Elizabeth Minnis, May 15, 1751.
B. Francis, son of Eleanor Minnis, Feb. 20, 1759.
M. John Minor of Brunswick Parish and Margaret Sumner of Overwharton Parish, Feb. 3, 1740/1.
M. Jane Minor and William Kelly, Mar. 30, 1758.
M. Henry Mintoe of Overwharton Parish and Lurena Ward of this Parish, Jan. 16, 1737/8.

M. Priscilla Mirax and Joshua Sebastian, Mar. 10, 1748/9.
M. Anthony Mislin and Elizabeth Day of Strother's Parish, May 5, 1735.
M. William Mitchell and Behethland Johnson, Sept. 4, 1787.
M. Elizabeth Mizing and Richard Harmon, Mar. 28, 1746.
B. Mary, dau. of George and Jane Monk, Aug. 8, 1716.
D. Sarah, dau. of George and Jane Monk, Sept. 24, 1716.
M. William Monroe and Jemima Smith of Washington Parish, Apr. 2, 1746.
M. Andrew Monroe and Margaret Washington, Dec. 21, 1761.
M. Mary Monroe and Price Thomas, Nov. 7, 1779.
M. Anne Monroe and Jeremiah Kirk, Aug. 18, 1785.
M. James Monteith and Leah Owens, Aug. 23, 1763.
M. Richard Moody and Elizabeth Townley, Feb. 5, 1758.
B. John, son of Richard and Elizabeth Moody, Jan. 19, 1759.
B. Margaret, dau. of Richard and Elizabeth Moody, Feb. 14, 1761.
M. Anne Moody and William Purchase, July 3, 1775.
M. Elizabeth More and Leonard Martin, Dec. 28, 1764.
D. John Morgan, Feb. 10, 1730/1.
M. Edward Morris (Morning?) and Catherine Greenleves, Oct. 16, 1779.
B. James Morton, Mar. 21, 1733/4.
M. Patrick Morrow and Mary Delander, Oct. 6, 1716.
D. Mary, dau. of John Moss, Aug. 15, 1716.
D. Catherine Moss, Apr. 1, 1716.
B. William, son of William and Margaret Moss, Mar. 10, 1717/8.
B. Jane, dau. of John and Elizabeth Moss, Apr. 7, 1718.
B. Jane, dau. of Thomas Moss, dec'd., and Mary his wife, Nov. 16, 1719.
D. Sarah, dau. of John Moss, May 1, 1720.
D. Robert, son of John Moss, May 18, 1720.
D. Jane, dau. of Mary Moss, Nov. 14, 1720.
B. Sarah, dau. of John and Elizabeth Moss, Sept. 17, 1722.
M. Jane Moss and John Kelly, Dec. 21, 1722.
D. John Moss, Aug. 20, 1723.
B. William Moss's child, Dec. 30, 1723.
M. John Moss and Mary Ross, Apr. 27, 1724.
M. Mary Moss and John Taylor, Aug. 19, 1724.
D. Elizabeth, dau. of Thomas and Mary Moss, Oct. 27, 1724.
B. Rae, son of John and Mary Moss, June 27, 1725.
B. Jesse, son of William and Margaret Moss, Mar. 3, 1725/6.
B. Jean, dau. of John and Mary Moss, June 14, 1727.
D. Jean, dau. of John and Mary Moss, June 15, 1727.
M. Sylvester Moss and Frances Kelly, July 7, 1727.
B. Margaret, dau. of John and Margaret Moss, Aug. 1, 1727.
D. Frances Moss, June 4, 1729.
B. Elizabeth, dau. of William and Margaret Moss, Apr. 10, 1731.
B. Thomas, son of William and Margaret Moss, Oct. 3, 1733.
M. Sylvester Moss and Elizabeth Reid, Aug. 25, 1735.
D. John Moss, Nov. 1, 1735.
B. Francis, son of William and Margaret Moss, Jan. 30, 1735/6.
M. Mary Moss and Nicholas Savin, May 5, 1736.
B. Anne, dau. of Sylvester and Elizabeth Moss, Oct. 1, 1736.
B. Elizabeth, dau. of Sylvester and Elizabeth Moss, Dec. 15, 1737.[47]
B. Margaret, dau. of William and Margaret Moss, Nov. 15, 1738.
B. Moses, son of Sylvester and Elizabeth Moss, Feb. 13, 1738/9.
M. Alice Moss and Richard Sebastian, June 1, 1742.
B. Peggy, dau. of William and Elizabeth Moss, Feb. 16, 1743/4.
M. Eleanor Moss and John Jones, Aug. 16, 1744.
B. William, son of William and Elizabeth Moss, May 17, 1746.

D. William Moss (Sr.) Feb. 13, 1745/6.
B. John, son of William and Elizabeth Moss, June 9, 1751.
B. Elizabeth, dau. of William and Elizabeth Moss, Dec. 22, 1753.
M. Jane Moss and Benjamin Rogers, Jan. 27, 1761.
M. Thomas Moss and Mary Atwell, Sept. 10, 1772.
M. Alvin Moxley and Anne Hooe, Nov. 5, 1772.
B. Anne Dent, dau. of Alvin and Anne Moxley, Aug. 31, 1773.
M. Peggy Mundy and Robert Clift, Jan. 6, 1793.
B. Grace, dau. of John and Jane Murphy, Apr. 24, 1716.
D. Jane, wife of John Murphy, Jan. 6, 1717/8.
M. Helen Murphy and Thomas Williams, Sept. 4, 1723.
D. John Murphy, Jan. 30, 1723/4.
M. Alexander Murphy and Anne Darbin, Apr. 8, 1724.
B. Frances, dau. of Alexander and Anne Murphy, Feb. 21, 1725/6.
B. Thomas Murphy, Feb. 5, 1729/30.
B. Sarah, dau. of Alexander and Anne Murphy, Oct. 24, 1731.
B. John, son of John and Margaret Murphy, July 2, 1749.
M. William Lewis Murphy and Elizabeth Smith, Apr. 5, 1768.
M. John Murray and Mary Todd, Dec. 12, 1727.
M. Elizabeth Mustin and John Gordon, Nov. 24, 1747.
M. Thomas Mustin and Anne Martin, Jan. 19, 1759.
B. William, son of Thomas and Anne Mustin, Apr. 5, 1760.
B. John, son of Thomas and Anne Mustin, Aug. 3, 1761.
B. Sarah, dau. of Thomas and Anne Mustin, May 3, 1765 (1764).
B. Margaret, dau. of Thomas and Anne Mustin, Jan. 5, 1766.
B. Thomas, son of Thomas and Anne Mustin, Oct. 17, 1767.
B. Leonard, son of Thomas and Anne Mustin, Feb. 1, 1772.
B. James, son of Thomas and Anne Mustin, Feb. 3, 1774.

N

B. Susanna, dau. of Robert and Esther Nash, Aug. 2, 1746.
M. George Nash and Anne White, Jan. 20, 1769.
B. Katherine Naughton, Sept. 3, 1743.
M. Elizabeth Naylor of Brunswick Parish and John Simpson of Overwharton
   Parish, Aug. 6, 1735.[48]
M. Mary Neale and Benjamin Derrick, Sept. 30, 1729.
D. George Neagle, a servant of George Monk, Oct. 17, 1718.
M. Sarah Neale and Joshua Sawyer, June 24, 1732.
M. Anne Neaps and William Skinner, Aug. 20, 1767.
M. Elizabeth Netherington and William Walker, Nov. 23, 1731.
M. David Nevins and Janet Patterson, June 6, 1759.
B. Mary, dau. of David and Janet Nevins, June 3, 1764.
B. Janet, dau. of David and Janet Nevins, Aug. 27, 1765.
M. David Nevins and Mary Clark, June 28, 1767.
M. Zachariah Newble and Anne Hammit, Nov. 6, 1779.
M. James Newman and Sarah Griffin, Dec. 25, 1759.
M. Elizabeth Newport and Simon Bowling, June 5, 1728.
D. Mary Newton, Mar. 25, 1716.
M. Benjamin Newton and Elizabeth Nicholson, May 6, 1716.
M. Anne Newton and Simon Bowling, Dec. 5, 1722.
M. Elizabeth Newton and Thomas Stribling, Dec. 7, 1725.
M. Sarah Newton and William Higgins, Dec. 9, 1732.
M. Benjamin Newton of Hamilton Parish and Jane Colclough, Oct. 22, 1740.
M. Elizabeth Nicholson and Benjamin Newton, May 6, 1716.
D. Mary Nicholson, May 13, 1722.

M. Margaret Noling and Benjamin Mehorner, Apr. 5, 1778.
M. Thomas Norfolk and Mary Burkett, Dec. 6, 1737.
B. John, son of Thomas and Mary Norfolk, Jan. 4, 1740/1.
M. Thomas Norman and Elizabeth Duncomb, Feb. 21, 1736/7.
M. Anne Norman and Jesse Briant, Jan. 1, 1790.
M. John Norris and Sarah Turner, Aug. 29, 1751.
M. William Norton and Margaret Hamilton, Feb. 26, 1724/5.
D. Margaret Norton, Jan. 29, 1725/6.
B. William, son of Peter and Anne Noshard, May 15, 1758.
D. Thomas Nowland, a servant boy of Daniel Mealy, July 29, 1718.
M. Peter Nugent and Martha Sill, both of Hanover Parish, Feb. 15, 1731/2.[49]

O

M. John Oakley and Anne Gordon, Feb. 14, 1744/5.
M. William Oakley and Mildred Sullivan, Feb. 4, 1781.
D. John Oliver, Mar. 5, 1715/6.
B. John, son of John and Margaret Oliver, Feb. 15, 1720/1.
B. Elias, son of John and Margaret Oliver, Feb. 19, 1723/4.
D. Nathaniel, and John Oliver, children, suddenly, Nov. 20, 1725.
D. Sarah Oliver, Jan. 30, 1725/6.
B. George, son of John and Margaret Oliver, Jan. 29, 1726/7.
B. George, son of John and Elizabeth Oliver, Jan. 15, 1727/8.
B. Margaret, dau. of John and Margaret Oliver, Jan. 3, 1732/3.
B. John, son of John and Margaret Oliver, Oct. 18, 1735.
B. Mary, dau. of John and Margaret Oliver, Apr. 7, 1738.
D. Mary, dau. of John and Margaret Oliver, May 28, 1740.
B. Rebecca, dau. of John and Margaret Oliver, Sept. 29, 1741.
M. George Oliver and Jemima Regan, Aug. 1, 1745.
M. Margaret Oliver and Nathaniel Higdon (Hogdon?), Mar. 2, 1746/7.
M. Rebecca Oliver and William Mehony, Sept. 15, 1759.
B. John, son of John and Mildred Oliver, July 14, 1760.
B. Elisha, son of John and Mildred Oliver, Apr. 26, 1768.
B. Sarah, dau. of John and Mildred Oliver, Oct. 1, 1772.
M. Nancy Oliver and James Giles, Mar. 24, 1788.
M. Mary Oneal and John Ellis, Sept. 17, 1722.
D. Mary Oneal, Nov. 12, 1730.
B. William son of Mary Ore (Orr?), Sept. 2, 1760.
M. Elinor Ormand and John Conali, June 13, 1725.
M. Mary Orr and David Cable, Sept. 7, 1766.
D. Thomas Osburn, Oct. 18, 1728.
B. Frances, dau. of William and Mary Overall, Aug. 22, 1716.
D. Jane, mother of William Overall, Apr. 5, 1718.
M. John Overall and Mary Ellis, Oct. 8, 1722.
D. William Overall, Jan. 17, 1725/6.
B. Sarah, dau. of John and Mary Overall, Feb. 7, 1725/6.
M. Mary Overall and Anthony Kitchen, Aug. 31, 1727.
M. Sarah Overall and John Dagg, Nov. 14, 1729.
B. Mary, dau. of John and Mary Overall, Mar. 19, 1730/1.
M. Elizabeth Overall of this Parish and John Whitledge of Hamilton Parish,
        Sept. 15, 1733.
M. Frances Overall of this Parish and Nathaniel Whitledge of Hamilton Parish,
        Parish, Oct. 27, 1733.
M. Sarah Overall and Joseph Powell, Sept. 21, 1750.
M. Mary Overall and James Bowling, Feb. 11, 1750/1.
M. Behethland Overall and James Cunningham, June 21, 1757.

B. John, son of Susanna Owens, Feb. 13, 1745/6.
M. Susanna Owens and Thomas Timmons, May 14, 1749.
M. Leah Owens and James Monteith, Aug. 23, 1763.
B. Essena, dau. of Aaron Owens, Nov. 30, 1767.
B. William, son of John and Dulcibella Owens, Sept. 21, 1768.
M. Lucinda Owens and Thomas Jett, Jan. 12, 1775.
M. Jane Owens and James Staples, Feb. 12, 1778.
M. Aaron Owens and Catherine Wilson, Mar. 26, 1785.
M. Aaron Owens and Amie Mannard, May 13, 1791.
M. Letty Owens and Eli Mehorner, June 23, 1792.
M. Elizabeth Oxford and Richard Thomson, June 3, 1724.
M. Elizabeth Oxford and Samuel Bowling, Oct. 8, 1731.
B. John, son of Samuel and Mary Oxford, Nov. 3, 1731.
B. Anne, dau. of Samuel and Mary Oxford, Dec. 28, 1733.
B. Elizabeth, dau. of Samuel and Mary Oxford, Aug. 7, 1736.
M. Edward Oxiven and Eleanor Dunfee, Nov. 27, 1724.

P

B. Isabel, dau. of John and Mary Palmer, Sept. 12, 1740.
M. Thomas Parcmane and Mary Lacy, Aug. 28, 1751.
M. James Park and Sally Dade, Mar. 4, 1796.
D. John Parsons, Dec. 9, 1732.
M. David Parsons and Elizabeth Jones, Feb. 25, 1759.
M. Janet Patterson and David Nevins, June 6, 1759.
M. John Patton and Martha Payne of Hanover Parish, Apr. 3, 1746.
M. Frances Paulet and William Staples, Feb. 18, 1790.
D. Richard Payne, Apr. 21, 1721.
D. William Payne, Jan. 14, 1731/2.
M. Sarah Payne and John Lackey, June 6, 1737.
M. Martha Payne of Hanover Parish and John Patton, Apr. 3, 1746.
M. Jeremiah Payne and Judith Duke, May 25, 1760.
B. Mary, dau. of William Payne, Sept. 8, 1764.
B. Sarah, dau. of Susanna Payne, Aug. 7, 1765.
B. Rice, son of Virgin Payne, Aug. 28, 1766.
B. Frank, son of Francis and Anne Payne, Dec. 1, 1765.
B. Elias, son of Susanna Payne, Mar. 10, 1767.
B. John, son of William and Elizabeth Payne, Apr. 15, 1769.
B. John, son of Virgin Payne, Oct. 13, 1772.
B. Mary Anne, dau. of William Peake, Feb. 12, 1757.
M. Frances Peake and Benjamin Clift, Feb. 16, 1772.
M. Susanna Pearson and John Alexander, Dec. 15, 1734.
M. Elizabeth Peck and Thomas Stribling, Mar. 8, 1752.
M. William Peck and Jane Curry, Aug. 3, 1766.
B. Sarah, dau. of William and Jane Peck, Aug. 28, 1767.
B. Stribling, son of William and Jane Peck, Sept. 27, 1768.
B. Mildred, dau. of William and Jane Peck, May 21, 1771.
B. Robert, son of William and Jane Peck, June 14, 1772.
B. David, son of William and Jane Peck, Apr. 11, 1773.
B. John, son of Reuben and Eleanor Peck, Dec. 3, 1773.
B. Francis, son of James and Anne Peed, Jan. 15, 1738/9.
D. Philip, son of James and Anne Peed, Oct. 3, 1740.
M. John Peed and Behethland Jones, Feb. 14, 1770.
B. Mildred, dau. of John and Behethland Peed, Sept. 22, 1772.
M. Joanna Peed and Rush Marshall, Nov. 23, 1779.
M. Dolly Peed and John White, Jan. 3, 1790.
D. Robert Pennuel, husband of Thomasin Pennuel, Mar. 20, 1717/8.

M. Elizabeth Pennuel and Thomas Vincent, Apr. 3, 1749.
B. James, son of James and Alce Penny, Feb. 2, 1732/3.
B. Sarah, dau. of James and Alce Penny, Jan. 10, 1734/5.
B. William, son of Simon and Martha Perry, May 2, 1744.
B. Susanna, dau. of Simon and Martha Perry, Sept. 10, 1749.
B. Elisha, son of Simon and Martha Perry, Feb. 26, 1752.
B. Simon, son of Simon and Martha Perry, Jan. 12, 1756.
M. Elisha Perry and Gracey Waugh, Jan. 30, 1783.
M. Simon Perry and Anne Hartley, Dec. 25, 1783.
M. John Perry and Anne Massey, May 26, 1785.
M. Simon Perry and Elizabeth Fountain, Feb. 16, 1791.
M. Henry Peyton and Susanna Fowke, Mar. 15, 1764.
M. Carnaby Peyton and Mary Wilton, July 5, 1764.[50]
M. Francis Peyton and Frances Dade, Apr. 24, 1755.
M. Mary Pew and Ephraim Simmons, Apr. 13, 1740.
M. John Philips and Mary Edwards, Feb. 27, 1737/8.
M. Thomas Philips and Priscilla Bolling, Apr. 13, 1760.
M. Thomas Philips and Isabel Holland, June 14, 1772.
M. Charles Philips and Dully Carver, Aug. 19, 1787.
M. Elizabeth Philips and James Grisset, May 19, 1791.
B. John, son of William and Elizabeth Pickett, Feb. 26, 1734/5.
B. Martin, son of William and Elizabeth Pickett, Dec. 25, 1736.
B. William, son of Stephen and Jane Pilcher, Mar. 3, 1716/5 (?)
D. John Pilcher, Jan. 16, 1735/6.
M. Jane Pilcher and David Bowling, Sept. 10, 1741.
M. Judith Pilcher of Hanover Parish and John Campbell, Aug. 20, 1746.[51]
M. John Pimm (?Primm) and Ruth Finchum, Dec. 29, 1760.
M. Elizabeth Plunket of Hanover Parish and John Willis, Jan. 17, 1734/5.
D. Lancelot Pockley, Sept. 24, 1736.
M. Lucinda Pollard and William Bruce, Dec. 20, 1787.
M. Anne Poplar and Maurice (Morris?) Cunningham, Apr. 2, 1738.
B. Anne, dau. of Thomas and Anne Porter, Oct. 13, 1717 and baptized Nov. 17.
M. Mary Porter and William Toul, Oct. 15, 1722.
Bapt. Benjamin, son of Thomas and Anne Porter, May 1, 1725.
B. Joseph, son of Thomas and Anne Porter, Aug. 7, 1727.
D. Anne Porter, Sept. 22, 1727.
B. Anne, dau. of Thomas and Anne Porter, Mar. 15, 1731/2 and baptized Apr. 30, 1732.[52]
B. John, son of Thomas and Anne Porter, Aug. 4, 1734 and baptized Oct. 6.
M. Parthenia Posey and Rawleigh Dye, May 7, 1790.
B. Richard, son of William and Honor Potes, ...1724.
D. William Potes, Feb. 21, 1733/4.
M. Honor Potes and James Rea, July 2, 1738.
B. Sarah, dau. of Richard and Elizabeth Potes, Dec. 21, 1771.
M. Susanna Potter and Daniel Fitzhugh, Oct. 24, 1772.
D. William, son of William and Amy Powell, Oct. 30, 1716.
D. Joseph, brother of William Powell, Dec. 19, 1717.
B. Elizabeth, dau. of William and Amy Powell, Nov. 17, 1717.
B. John, son of William and Amy Powell, Aug. 16, 1720.
M. Jane Powell and Elijah Wood, June 30, 1722.
M. Grace Powell and James Berry, May 28, 1723.
B. Joan, dau. of William and Amy Powell, June 20, 1725.
D. Richard Powell, Jan. 15, 1725/6.
D. Elizabeth, dau. of William and Amy Powell, Sept. 27, 1728.
M. Jemima Powell and Edward Derrick, Jan. 2, 1728/9.
M. Frances Powell and John Johnson, Nov. 18, 1731.

B. Richard, son of William and Amy Powell, June 1, 1733.
D. Grace Powell, Oct. 29, 1734.
M. Elizabeth Powell and John Massey, June 12, 1736.
B. Amy, dau. of William and Amy Powell, Sept. 10, 1736.
M. Katherine Powell and Benjamin Derrick, July 29, 1737.
B. Elisha, son of William and Amy Powell, May 2, 1739.
D. John, son of William and Amy Powell, Nov. 27, 1739.
D. Jane, dau. of Wm. and Amy Powell, Jan. 2, 1739/40.
D. Richard, son of William and Amy Powell, Dec. 27, 1742.
D. William Powell, Jan. 20, 1745/6.
M. William Powell and Elizabeth Regan, Apr. 2, 1747.
M. Joseph Powell and Sarah Overall, Sept. 21, 1750.
B. Elizabeth, dau. of Joseph and Mary Powell, Dec. 13, 1751.
M. Amy Powell and Anthony Buckner Thomas, Apr. 20, 1755.
B. Jane, dau. of Joseph and Sarah Powell, Dec. 15, 1753.
B. William, son of Joseph and Sarah Powell, May 5, 1756.
B. John, son of Joseph and Sarah Powell, Dec. 28, 1758.
M. Elisha Powell and Winifred Massey, Dec. 20, 1761.
M. James Power and Mary Lewis, Oct. 19, 1724.
D. Elizabeth Power, June 27, 1725.
M. Elizabeth Powers of Caroline and James Cough (Gouch?) Feb. 21, 1762.
D. John Pratt, Feb. 12, 1737.
B. Susanna, dau. of Thomas and Margaret Pratt, Feb. 8, 1756.
B. Molly, dau. of Thomas and Margaret Pratt, Jan. 28, 1758.
B. John Burkett, son of Thomas Pratt, Aug. 1, 1761.
B. Thomas, son of Thomas and Margaret Pratt, June 20, 1765.
M. Margaret Pratt and Bernard Hooe, Nov. 2, 1771.
M. Mildred Pratt and Henry Washington, March 12, 1779.
M. Susanna Pratt and William Hooe, Nov. 13, 1782.
M. Thomas Pratt and Jane Brockenburg, June 23, 1785.
D. Thomasin Prestridge, Nov. 1, 1725.
B. Alse, dau. of Thomas and Anne Prestridge, Oct. 12, 1726.
M. Thomas Prestridge and Eleanor Mastin, Dec. 29, 1726.
B. - - - Prestridge, Feb. 3, 1729/30.
D. Thomas Prestridge, Mar. 22, 1731/2.
B. Thomas, son of Thomas and Anne Prestridge, Feb. 23, 1732/3.
B. Elizabeth, dau. of Thomas and Anne Prestridge, Mar. 4, 1734/5.
D. Thomas Prestridge, Apr. 9, 1737.
M. Anne Prestridge and William Steele, Apr. 27, 1742.
B. William, son of (Thomas and?) Sarah Prestridge, Feb. 11, 1750/1.
B. Linny, dau. of Thomas and Sarah Prestridge, Dec. 12, 1756.
M. Sarah Prestridge and Reuben Bates, Dec. 4, 1757.
M. Michael Price and Anne Dennis, Aug. 24, 1727.
M. Mary Price and Massey Thomas, Nov. 28, 1731.
M. Thomas Price and Sarah Buckner, Dec. 31, 1734.
B. Anthony, son of Thomas and Sarah Price, Nov. 12, 1736.
B. Anne, dau. of Thomas and Sarah Price, Dec. 20, 1738.
B. Margaret, dau. of Thomas and Sarah Price, Feb. 10, 1737/8.
B. Merryday (Meredith?), son of Thomas (and Sarah?) Price, Sept. 5, 1739.
B. Elizabeth, dau. of Thomas and Sarah Price, June 3, 1741.
B. Sarah, dau. of Thomas and Sarah Price, May 13, 1743.
B. Katherine, dau. of Thomas and Sarah Price, Feb. 7, 1744/5.
M. Nathaniel Price and Jane Blankenship, July 25, 1746.
B. Susanna, dau. of Thomas and Sarah Price, Mar. 20, 1746/7.
B. John, son of Thomas and Sarah Price, June 3, 1749.
B. Mary, dau. of William and Sarah Price, Jan. 1, 1754.[53]

M. Elizabeth Price and Moses Burgess, May 30, 1762.
M. Mary (?) Price and Edward Burgess, Feb. 20, 1765.
M. Anthony Price and Elizabeth Stribling, Jan. 17, 1768.
B. Sarah, dau. of Anthony and Elizabeth Price, July 27, 1769.
B. Thomas, son of Anthony and Elizabeth Price, Mar. 31, 1772.
B. Buckner, son of Anthony and Elizabeth Price, Sept. 21, 1774.
M. Molly Price and James Williams, Apr. 24, 1782.
M. John Price and Susanna Jones, May 5, 1786.
M. Sally Price and Benjamin Roach, Dec. 22, 1766.
M. Mary Price and Moses Mardus, Feb. 27, 1791.
D. Frances Prosser, Sept. 4, 1732.
D. Anthony Prosser, Mar. 5, 1732/3.
M. Pemberton Proudlove and Alse Ware, Feb. 10, 1717/8.
D. Pemberton Proudlove, Oct. 22, 1725.
M. Alice (Alse?) Proudlove and Christopher Bell, June 4, 1726.
M. Peter Puckett and Amie Keith, Dec. 27, 1775.
M. William Purchase and Anne Moody, July 3, 1775.
M. Elizabeth Purtle and Joseph Crismund, Feb. 16, 1752.

Q

M. William Quarles and Lucy Alexander, Oct. 20, 1784.

R

M. Sarah Radford and Michael Black, Dec. 3, 1752.
M. Anne Ramsey and Richard Dixon, Apr. 13, 1775.
M. Nicholas Randolph and Margaret Reddish, Feb. 21, 1733/4.
D. Thomas Randolph, Dec. 16, 1735.
M. William Randolph and Mary Grymes, May 18, 1770.
M. Robert Rankins and Jane Fingleston, Dec. 26, 1756.
M. Mary Rankins and Henry Ward, June 14, 1775.
D. James Ranton, July 25, 1717.
M. Judith Rawlings and Thomas Lacy, Nov. 9, 1716.
B. Kidwell, son of William and Elizabeth Rawlings, Mar. 19, 1726/7.
M. Mary Rawlings and William Baxter, Apr. 1, 1735.
B. John, son of Thomas and Mary Rawlings, Mar. 13, 1742/3.
B. Joseph, son of Thomas and Mary Rawlings, Feb. 15, 1744/5.
M. Richard Rawlings and Katherine Rice of Washington Parish, Apr. 11, 1746.
M. Rebecca Rawlings and Archibald Campbell, Jan. 15, 1753.
M. James Rawlings and Margaret Stribling, Jan. 5, 1778.
M. Joseph Rawlings and Elizabeth Mardus, May 25, 1778.
M. Sarah Rawlings and Thomas Gutridge, May 16, 1782.
M. Margaret Rawlings and William Hudson, Mar. 10, 1785.
M. John Raymond and Katherine Campbell, Jan. 12, 1735/6.
B. Richard, son of John and Katherine Raymond, Oct. 20, 1736.
B. John, son of John and Katherine Raymond, Dec. 7, 1738.
B. Mary, dau. of John and Katherine Raymond, Nov. 15, 1740.
D. Katherine, wife of John Raymond, Jan. 8, 1743/4.
M. John Raymond and Margaret Robertson, Feb. 27, 1746/7.
D. Mary, wife of James Rea, Nov. 6, 1737.
M. James Rea and Honor Potes, July 2, 1738.
D. James Rea, Sept. 4, 1740.
B. Elizabeth, dau. of Charles and Elizabeth Reagan, Oct. 20, 1731.
B. Katherine, dau. of Charles and Elizabeth Reagan, July 25, 1733.
D. Katherine, dau. of Charles and Elizabeth Reagan, Feb. 1, 1734/5.

B. John, son of Charles and Elizabeth Reagan, Aug. 23, 1736.
B. James, son of Charles and Elizabeth Reagan, Apr. 9, 1738.
B. Elisha, son of Charles and Elizabeth Reagan, Apr. 19, 1740.
B. Mary, dau. of James and Elizabeth Reddish, May 5, 1721.[54]
M. Sarah Reddish and John Gordon, Jan. 24, 1722/3.
M. Catherine Reddish and William Vaint, Aug. 27, 1723.
M. James Reddish and Elizabeth Massey, Aug. 19, 1726.
M. Robert Reddish and Helen Durham, Nov. 10, 1727.
B. Mary, dau. of Robert and Elinor (Helen?) Reddish, Feb. 28, 1731/2.
M. Margaret Reddish and Nicholas Randolph, Feb. 21, 1733/4.
B. John, son of Robert (and Helen?) Reddish, Aug. 20, 1734.[55]
M. Robert Reddish and Jane Allerton, Oct. 12, 1735.[55]
B. Joel, son of Joseph and Sarah Reddish, Feb. 22, 1747/8.
B. Winifred, dau. of Joseph and Sarah Reddish, Aug. 26, 1749.
B. Behethland, dau. of Joseph and Sarah Reddish, Aug. 25, 1751.
B. Sadyris, dau. of Joseph and Sarah Reddish, Mar. 21, 1754.
B. Eleanor, dau. of Joseph and Sarah Reddish, Mar. 3, 1759.
D. Matthew Regan, Mar. 30, 1716.
B. Winifred, dau. of Bridget Regan, May 16, 1744.
D. William Regan, Nov. 21, 1744.
M. Jemima Regan and George Oliver, Aug. 1, 1745.
B. Isaac, son of Margaret Regan, Dec. 22, 1746.
M. Elizabeth Regan and William Powell, Apr. 2, 1747.
M. Margaret Regan and Jacob Johnson, Oct. 13, 1748.
M. Charles Regg and Sarah Day of Hanover Parish, July 17, 1746.
M. Elizabeth Reid and Sylvester Moss, Aug. 25, 1735.
B. John, son of Thomas and Elizabeth Reilly, Sept. 17, 1716.
B. Phillis, dau. of Thomas and Elizabeth Reilly, Nov. 14, 1717.
B. Anne, dau. of Thomas and Elizabeth Reilly, Jan. 19, 1720/1.
M. Margaret Reiney and James Stuart, Mar. 24, 1724/5.
B. John, son of Jane Reiney, Mar. 7, 1748/9.
M. Jane Reiney and William Jones, Apr. 20, 1752.
B. Anne, dau. of Thomas and Elizabeth Remy, Jan. 11, 1720/1.
B. John, son of Hugh and Mary Rice, July 26, 1716.
M. Katherine Rice of Washington Parish and Richard Rawlings, Apr. 11, 1746.
M. Frances Richards and Horatio Dade, Oct. 5, 1749.
M. William Richardson and Clary Mannard, Jan. 16, 1791.
B. Anne, dau. of Alexander and Anne Rigby, Dec. 3, 1720.
B. Elizabeth, dau. of Alexander and Anne Rigby, Apr. 10, 1722.
B. Sarah, dau. of Alexander and Anne Rigby, Mar. 20, 1727/8.
M. Alexander Rigby and Jane Johnson, Dec. 28, 1729.
M. Mary Rigsby and Thomas Robins, July 16, 1742.
D. Elizabeth, dau. of William and Elizabeth Bridget Riggins, Oct. 7, 1717.
B. John, son of William and Elizabeth Bridget Riggins, Nov. 3, 1717.
D. John, son of William and Elizabeth Bridget Riggins, Sept. 12, 1718.
B. Peter, son of William and Elizabeth Bridget Riggins, Apr. 10, 1722.
D. Elizabeth, dau. of Wm. and Elizabeth Bridget Riggins, Oct. 7, 1723.
B. Keziah, dau. of William and Elizabeth Bridget Riggins, Feb. 2, 1726/7.
B. Elizabeth, dau. of William and Elizabeth Bridget Riggins, Apr. 20, 1731.
B. Bridget, dau. of William and Elizabeth Bridget Riggins, June 22, 1733.[56]
D. Bridget Riggins, June 22, 1733.
M. Jane Riggins and Samuel Evans, June 29, 1746.
M. Keziah Riggins and Alexander Douglas, May 2, 1749.
M. Benjamin Roach and Sally Price, Dec. 22, 1786.
B. Mary, dau. of Katherine Roane, Mar. 6, 1739/40.
M. Mary Robbins and Timothy Barrington, Oct. 15, 1731.

M. Thomas Robbins and Mary Rigsby, July 16, 1742.
M. Margaret Robertson and John Raymond, Feb. 17, 1746/7.
B. Sarah, dau. of Margaret Robertons (Robinson?), Dec. 27, 1745.
D. John Robinson, June 21, 1725.
B. Anne, dau. of Edward and Bridget Roddy, May 27, 1743.
B. James, son of Edward and Mary Roddy, Jan. 20, 1744/5.
M. Bartholomew Rodman and Joan Elkins, June 24, 1727.
M. Sarah Roe and John Skinner, Sept. 15, 1743.
M. Mary Rogers and William Colclough, Dec. 30, 1741.
B. Rice, son of William and Frances Rogers, June 17, 1746.
B. Behethland, dau. of William and Frances Rogers, Mar. 13, 1747/8.
M. Joseph Rogers and Anne Burgess, Oct. 24, 1749.
B. Anne, dau. of Grigsby and Grace Rogers, Oct. 13, 1750.
B. Mary, dau. of Grigsby and Mary Rogers, Mar. 30, 1752.
B. Robert, son of William and Frances Rogers, Oct. 9, 1753.
B. Margaret, dau. of William and Frances Rogers, Aug. 17, 1756.
B. Winifred, dau. of William and Frances Rogers, Mar. 21, 1759.
M. Benjamin Rogers and Jane Moss, Jan. 27, 1761.
M. Behethland Rogers and John Chandler, Sept. 17, 1767.
B. James, son of Benjamin and Jane Rogers, May 10, 1768.
M. Sarah Rogers and Benjamin Clift, Dec. 6, 1772.
M. Margaret Rogers and John Gordon, junr: Nov. 22, 1776.
M. Anne Rogers and John Clift, Sept. 29, 1779.
M. Susanna Rogers and Daniel Beattie, Aug. 2, 1781.
M. Hosea Rogers and Caty Clift, Jan. 22, 1783.
M. Anne Rogers and John Curry, Dec. 25, 1783.
M. James (?) Rogers and Elizabeth Wiggins, Aug. 12, 1787.
M. Isaac Rogers and Clarinda Lewis, Dec. 11, 1791.
B. Maxfield, son of William and Mary Rose, Nov. 27, 1717.
M. Pleasant Rose and John Smith, Sept. 30, 1725.
B. Francis, son of William and Mary Rose, Mar. 2, 1734/5.
M. William Rose and Sarah Day, June 6, 1737.
B. William, son of William and Sarah Rose, Dec. 5, 1737.
M. The Rev. Mr. Robert Rose of St. Anne's Parish and Anne Fitzhugh of this
     Parish, Nov. 6, 1740.
B. Elizabeth, dau. of William and Sarah Rose, Dec. 28, 1740.
B. Henry, son of the Rev. Mr. Robert Rose of Essex and Anne, his wife, Dec.
     20, 1741.
B. Hugh, son of the Rev. Robert and Anne Rose, Sept. 18, 1743.
B. Mary, dau. of William and Sarah Rose, Mar. 2, 1743/4.
M. Mary Rose and Richard Lee, June 29, 1744.
B. Patrick, son of Rev. Robert and Anne Rose, July 4, 1745.
B. Zachariah, son of William and Sarah Rose, June 2, 1747.
B. Charles, son of Rev. Robert and Anne Rose, Aug. 17, 1747.
B. William, son of Futral (?) and Anne Rose, Mar. 18, 1747/8.
M. Isaac Rose and Rachel Grigsby, Dec. 19, 1751.
M. Robert Rose and Frances Jones, June 7, 1752.[57]
B. Elizabeth, dau. of Margaret Rose, Dec. 24, 1753.
M. Francis Rose and Hester Stripling, May 31, 1756.
M. Jane Rose and Oswald Crismund, June 27, 1757.
B. William, son of Francis and Hester Rose, July 26, 1757.
M. Elias Rose and Sarah Sweeny, Sept. 2, 1758.
B. Isaac, son of William and Sarah Rose, Mar. 2, 1759.
B. Isaac, son of William and Sarah Rose, Jan. 20, 1761.
B. Anne, dau. of Francis and Mary Rose, Jan. 4, 1762.
M. Elizabeth Rose and Daniel Lewis, Aug. 31, 1762.

B. William, son of William and Sarah Rose, Feb. 20, 1764.
B. Bennett, son of Francis and Mary Rose, Mar. 18, 1766.
M. Mary Rose and John Carver, July 17, 1768.
B. John, son of Francis and Mary Rose, Oct. 22, 1768.
B. Anne, dau. of Caton and Mary Rose, July 4, 1774.
B. Joel Stripling, son of Francis and Mary Rose, Sept. 29, 1774.
M. John Rose and Anne Swillakeen, Jan. 4, 1776.
M. Zachariah Rose and Sarah Taylor, Mar. 19, 1778.
M. Elias Rose and Mary Brooke, Mar. 30, 1778.
M. Frances Rose and William Crysell, Nov. 17, 1782.
M. Mary Rose and Andrew Thompson, Jan. 2, 1787.
B. Sarah, dau. of Alexander and Elizabeth Ross, July 17, 1717.
D. Elizabeth Ross, Oct. 10, 1718.
D. Hugh Ross, Aug. 20, 1720.
M. Mary Ross and John Moss, Apr. 27, 1724.
B. William, son of Alexander and Sarah Ross, Feb. 8, 1726/7.
M. Isabel Ross and James Brown, June 4, 1726.
D. Alexander Ross, Nov. 14, 1728.
M. Sarah Ross and John Wilkinson, Nov. 13, 1730.
M. John Ross and Lucy Bennett, Oct. 14, 1731.
B. Bennett, son of John and Lucy Ross, Jan. 5, 1731/2.
D. Mary Ross, Jan. 17, 1735/6.
B. John, son of Jane Ross, Jan. 20, 1742/3.
M. Rachel Rosser of Hanover Parish and John Jackson, Jan. 31, 1731/2.
M. Susanna Roth and William Henson, Nov. 19, 1725.
M. Thomas Roy and Susanna Hooe, Sept. 7, 1777.
B. David, son of Hillaire and Elizabeth Rousseau, Nov. 2, 1717.
D. Hillaire Rousseau, June 30, 1720.
D. Simon Rutland, a child, Jan. 27, 1725/6.
D. Elizabeth, dau. of Thomas and Margaret Roy, Oct. 4, 1724.
D. John Rutland, Jan. 31, 1725/6.
M. Patrick Ryan and Elizabeth Edwards, May 6, 1723.
M. Mary Ryan and John Christie, May 4, 1749.
M. James Seaton Ryan and Jennet Bennett, Apr. 5, 1763.

S

M. Clement Sacheverel and Mary McIntosh, Aug. 11, 1751.
B. Elijah, son of Clement and Mary Sacheverel in Maryland, Aug. 30, 1757.
B. Elizabeth, dau. of Clement and Mary Sacheverel, Dec. 8, 1759.
B. Jane, dau. of Clement (and Mary?) Sacheverel, Aug. 25, 1763.
M. Clement Sacheverel and Eleanor Hodge, Nov. 8, 1763.
B. William, son of Clement and Mary (?) Sacheverel, Oct. 28, 1764.
B. Mary, dau. of Clement and Eleanor Sacheverel, July 29, 1766.
M. William Sacheverel and Elizabeth Tunnel, Feb. 26, 1784.
M. Mary Sacheverel and John Deacon, May 15, 1785.
M. Joanna Sacheverel and William Long, Dec. 30, 1790.
M. Sarah Sanders of St. Paul's and William Clark of Overwharton Parish, Aug. 5, 1752.
M. Samuel Sandys and Barbara Dagg, Sept. 12, 1724.
M. Joseph Sanford and Jane Bunbury, May 8, 1766.
M. Hannah Saunders and Thomas Horton, Feb. 10, 1786.
M. Nicholas Savin and Mary Moss, May 5, 1736.[58]
M. Joshua Sawyer (Lawyer?), and Sarah Neale, June 24, 1732.
D. Sophia Sawyer (Lawyer?), Mar. 13, 1733/4.
D. John Sawyer (Lawyer?), Mar. 19, 1733/4.

M. Sarah Sawyer and James Goodwin, June 5, 1735.
D. Edward Sawyer (Layer?), Jan. 17, 1739/40.
M. William Scapelan and Anne Holloway, Sept. 29, 1748.
M. William Scapelan and Mary Stewart, Feb. 21, 1754.
B. Joseph, son of William and Mary Scapelan, Oct. 8, 1757.
M. Catherine Schofield and George Stone, July 11, 1715.
M. William Scipier and Anne McFarland, Feb. 17, 1750/1.
M. William Scott and Anne Clifton, Feb. 23, 1727/8.
B. Elizabeth, dau. of William and Mary Scott, Feb. 28, 1727/8.
B. William, son of William and Anne Scott, Jan. 21, 1731/2.
B. Henry, son of William and Anne Scott, May 26, 1734.
B. Alexander, son of William and Anne Scott, Apr. 14, 1736.
B. Jannet, dau. of Dr. William Scott, Oct. 24, 1739.
D. Doctor William Scott, Sept. 17, 1742.
D. Anne, widow of Doctor William Scott, Sept. 11, 1743.
D. John Scott, Dec. 23, 1744.
M. William Scott and Mildred Bunbury, June 18, 1756.
B. John Mildred, son of William and Mildred Scott, Oct. 9, 1757.
M. Alexander Scott and Frances Bunbury, Feb. 22, 1758.
B. Francis, son of Alexander and Frances Scott, June 27, 1759.
M. William Scott and Sarah Gray, Apr. 18, 1765.
B. Anne, dau. of William and Sarah Scott, May 5, 1768.
B. James, son of William and Sarah Scott, Sept. 5, 1771.
B. Jane, dau. of William and Sarah Scott, Jan. 17, 1774.
M. John Mildred Scott and Mary Holland, Feb. 26, 1784.
M. John Scott and Dully Clift, Feb. 15, 1787.
M. James Scribner and Behethland Beach, Nov. 7, 1773.
B. Anne, dau. of William and Elizabeth Scudamore, Aug. 1, 1749.
B. Jane, dau. of James and Frances Seaton, Oct. 29, 1717.
B. George, son of James and Frances Seaton, Nov. 26, 1726.
D. Isaac Seaton, Dec. 10, 1725.
M. Elizabeth Seaton and John Lowry, Apr. 23, 1726.
D. Frances, wife of James Seaton, Dec. 12, 1730.
M. James Seaton and Grace Dounton, Mar. 11, 1730/1.
D. Jane Seaton, Jan. 31, 1735/6.
D. George Seaton, Feb. 21, 1735/6.
B. John, son of James and Grace Seaton, July 16, 1736.
B. George, son of James and Grace Seaton, Sept. 2, 1738.
M. Frances Seaton and Warriner Ford, July 24, 1740.
B. Jane, dau. of James and Grace Seaton, Apr. 17, 1741.
B. William, son of James and Grace Seaton, Oct. 4, 1743.
D. James Seaton, Sept. 20, 1744.
B. John, son of James and Frances Seaton, Jan. 12, 1744/5.
D. Frances, wife of James Seaton, Jan. 26, 1744/5.
M. Grace Seaton and Burdet Clifton, May 18, 1745.
M. Joseph Sebastian and Anne Martin, Feb. 6, 1717/8.
B. William, son of Joshua and Bethridge Sebastian, Jan. 18, 1720/1.
M. Anne Sebastian and John Allenthrope, Apr. 16, 1723.
B. Anne, dau. of Joseph and Anne Sebastian, Feb. 19, 1724/5.
B. Joshua, son of Joshua and Margaret Sebastian, Mar. 13, 1725/6.
B. Sarah, dau. of William and Elizabeth Sebastian, Sept. 1, 1726.
M. Nicholas Sebastian and Anne Elliott, Oct. 29, 1726.
M. Margaret Sebastian and Robert King, Apr. 26, 1727.
M. Isaac Sebastian and Rachel Spicer, May 11, 1727.
B. Joseph, son of Joseph and Anne Sebastian, Feb. 20, 1727/8.
M. Benjamin Sebastian and Priscilla Elkins, Feb. 16, 1729/30.

B. Rachel, dau. of Isaac and Rachel Sebastian, Jan. 6, 1730/1.
B. Thomas Elliott, son of Nicholas and Anne Sebastian, Mar. 20, 1730/1.
B. Hannah, dau. of Joshua and Margaret Sebastian, July 12, 1731.
B. Thaddeus, son of Joseph and Anne Sebastian, Mar. 9, 1731/2.
D. Thaddeus, son of Joseph and Anne Sebastian, Nov. 24, 1732.
B. Stephen, son of Isaac and Rachel Sebastian, Mar. 3, 1732/3.
B. Anne, dau. of Nicholas and Anne Sebastian, Mar. 2, 1733/4.
B. Elizabeth, dau. of Joseph and Anne Sebastian, Mar. 10, 1733/4.
B. Mary, dau. of Isaac and Rachel Sebastian, Apr. 20, 1734.
D. Elizabeth Sebastian, Oct. 12, 1734.
D. Stephen Sebastian, Feb. 7, 1734/5.
M. Margaret Sebastian and Joseph Sudduth, Oct. 13, 1735.
D. Joshua Sebastian, Feb. 24, 1734/5.
D. Nicholas Sebastian, Dec. 24, 1735.
M. Anne Sebastian and John James, Dec. 29, 1737.
M. Margaret Sebastian and Benjamin Clift, May 6, 1740.
M. Richard Sebastian and Alce Moss, June 1, 1742.
M. Mary Sebastian and William Johnson, Jan. 5, 1743/4.
B. Mary, dau. of Richard and Alice Sebastian, Apr. 30, 1744.
M. Jane Sebastian and David Jameson, May 7, 1744.
M. Rachel Sebastian and James Fletcher, Apr. 21, 1745.
B. Constant, dau. of Richard and Alice (Alce?) Sebastian, Sept. 16, and
        baptized Oct. 12, 1746.
M. Sarah Sebastian and Timothy Lyons (Lines?), Jan. 11, 1746/7.
M. Joshua Sebastian and Priscilla Mirax, Mar. 10, 1748/9.
B. Nicholas, son of Richard and Elizabeth Sebastian, Feb. 15, 1749/50.
M. Alice (Alse?) Sebastian and Andrew Allen, Feb. 12, 1750/1.[59]
M. Thomas Elliott Sebastian and Frances Embry, June 4, 1751.
M. Joseph Sebastian and Anne Coventry, Sept. 8, 1751.
M. Mary Sebastian and Benjamin Sudduth, Feb. 24, 1752.
M. Francis Selph and Elizabeth Gravat, Oct. 16, 1763.
M. John Selvie and Elizabeth Thomson, June 29, 1727.
M. Isaac Settle and Charity Brown, Sept. 24, 1726.
M. Elizabeth Settle of Hanover Parish and John McCormick, Mar. 8, 1735/6.
M. Verlinda Settle and Joel Ancrum, Sept. 12, 1745.
B. Henry, son of William and Hannah Settle, Sept. 20, 1769.
M. Thomas Settle and Elizabeth Wharton, Feb. 26, 1778.
M. Hannah Settle and William Massey, Feb. 8, 1784.
M. Elizabeth Settle and Thomas Tyler, Jan. 5, 1787.
M. Reuben Settle and Mary Taylor, June 15, 1792.
M. John Sevier (Pavier?) and Anne Awbry, June 1, 1738.
D. Thomas Sharpe's wife and child, Jan. 28, 1723/4.
D. Thomas Sharpe, Apr. 4, 1726.
D. Thomas Sharpe, Dec. 1, 1734.
M. Frances Sharpe of this Parish and John Kendall of Washington Parish, Sept.
        22, 1737.
D. John Sharpe, Feb. 3, 1741/2.
M. Sarah Sharpe and William Elliott, Dec. 17, 1752.
M. Elizabeth Sharpe and Vincent Kelly, Jan. 26, 1769.
M. Isaac Shepherd and Martha Greenslet, Feb. 17, 1749/50.
B. Margaret, dau. of Margaret Sherer, Mar. 12, 1736/7.
B. Patrick, son of Margaret Sherer, Sept. 14, 1741.
M. Margaret Sherer and Thomas Fletcher, Dec. 26, 1744.
M. Patrick Sherman and Anne Joy, Aug. 9, 1768.
B. John, son of Margaret Shipton, June 25, 1738.
B. Mary, dau. of John and Theodosia Short, Nov. 17, 1745.

B. Thomas, son of John and Theodosia Short, Feb. 9, 1746/7.
B. Sarah, dau. of John (and Theodosia?) Short, Jan. 14, 1748/9.
B. Elizabeth, dau. of John and Theodosia Short, July 8, 1757.
B. Anne, dau. of John and Theodosia Short, Jan. 17, 1760.
B. Thomas, son of John and Theodosia Short, Aug. 16, 1761.
B. John, son of John and Theodosia Short, May 8, 1763.
M. Mary Short and Benjamin Harrison, Nov. 17, 1770.
M. Sarah Short and Sigismund Massey, July 16, 1772.
M. Elizabeth Short and William Bunbury, Jan. 16, 1783.
M. John Shotwell and Sarah Worley, June 26, 1725.
B. Jeremiah, son of John and Sarah Shotwell, June 16, 1726.
M. Mary Shropshire of Hanover Parish and Joseph Smith, Apr. 3, 1746.
B. Thomas, son of Peter and Sarah Sidebottom, Jan. 7, 1736/7.
B. John (?), son of Peter and Sarah Sidebottom, Oct. 18, 1741.
B. William, son of Peter and Sarah Sidebottom, Aug. 17, 1743.
B. Charles, son of Peter and Sarah Sidebottom, Mar. 3, 1745/6.
B. Peter, son of Peter and Sarah Sidebottom, Apr. 9, 1748.
B. Anne, dau. of Peter and Sarah Sidebottom, Aug. 18, 1758.
B. Sarah, dau. of William and Elizabeth Sidebottom, June 8, 1767.
B. Thomas, son of William and Elizabeth Sidebottom, Feb. 19, 1769.
M. Martha Sill and Peter Nugent, both of Hanover Parish, Feb. 15, 1731/2.
B. Sarah, dau. of John and Jane Silver, Dec. 18, 1745.
D. John, son of Matthias and Elizabeth Simmons, Oct. 1, 1720.
B. Matthias, son of Matthias and Mary Simmons, Dec. 5, 1725.
M. Mary Simmons and Philip Crafford, Nov. 27, 1730.
M. Ephraim Simmons and Mary Pew, Apr. 13, 1740.
M. Duncan Simpson and Jane Dinsford, Dec. 27, 1732.
B. Samuel, son of Duncan and Jane Simpson, Mar. 7, 1734/5.
M. John Simpson of Overwharton Parish and Elizabeth Naylor of Brunswick
      Parish, Aug. 6, 1735.[60]
B. Duncan, son of Samuel and Lettice Simpson, Jan. 13, 1764.
B. Samuel Fetherington, son of Samuel (and Lettice?) Simpson, Dec. 15, 1765.
B. William, son of Samuel and Elizabeth Simpson, July 21, 1768.
M. Elizabeth Simpson and William Briant, June 21, 1779.
M. Samuel Sims and Sarah Mackall, July 10, 1735.
M. James Sims and Elizabeth Embry, Oct. 14, 1762.
M. Sarah Sims and James Baxter, Oct. 20, 1764.
B. Elisha, son of Mary Anne Sims, Mar. 26, 1766.
M. Victory Sims and Ambrose Deakins, May 24, 1789.
M. Sarah Skidmore and George Spicer, July 1, 1744.
B. Hannah, dau. of Jemima Skidmore, Mar. 19, 1746/7.
M. William Skidmore and Elizabeth Bowin, May 11, 1747.
M. Jemima Skidmore and Joseph Sudduth, Aug. 18, 1751.
M. Elizabeth Skidmore and John Burkett (Duckett?), Aug. 6, 1751.
M. Joshua Skidmore and Frances Bush, Aug. 6, 1751.
B. Sarah, dau. of Joshua and Frances Skidmore, Dec. 22, 1754.
D. William, son of Adam and Allin Skinner, June 20, 1716.
B. William, son of Adam and Catherine (Allin?) Skinner, Sept. 22, 1716.
B. Allin, dau. of Adam and Allin Skinner, Aug. 12, 1722.
M. Penelope Skinner and Archibald Allen, Dec. 26, 1722.
D. Allin, dau. of Adam and Allin Skinner, Sept. 19, 1722.
B. Mary, dau. of Adam and Katherine Skinner, ...1724.
BAPT. Thomas, son of Adam and Catherine Skinner, Apr. 9, 1727.
B. Katherine, dau. of Adam and Katherine Skinner, Apr. 5, 1732.
B. William, son of Katherine Skinner, Apr. 19, 1737.
M. Katherine Skinner and Thomas Adams, Oct. 18, 1738.

M. John Skinner and Sarah Roe, Sept. 15, 1743.
B. Thomas, son of John and Sarah Skinner, Nov. 9, 1746.
B. Henry Savin, son of John and Sarah Skinner, Sept. 26, 1749.
M. Thomas Skinner and Mary Elliott, Dec. 26, 1749.
B. John, son of John and Sarah Skinner, Jan. 30, 1752.
M. William Skinner and Anne Neaps, Aug. 30, 1767.
M. Adah Skinner and John Sullivan, Apr. 17, 1788.
M. Leah Skinner and Henry Mehorner, Sept. 13, 1788.
M. Zilpah Skinner and Thomas Truslow, Jan. 19, 1789.
M. James Smallwood and Frances Sweeny, May 23, 1776.
B. Mary, dau. of John and Charity Smith, Nov. 11, 1716.
M. John Smith and Mary Ancrum, Feb. 17, 1717/8.
D. Sarah Smith, Sept. 7, 1722.
B. Mary, dau. of John and Sarah Smith (dec'd.), Sept. 7, 1722.
M. Anne Smith and Richard Wilson, Oct. 31, 1722.
M. John Smith and Mary Duncan, Nov. 15, 1722.
M. Henry Smith and Margaret Christie, May 28, 1723.
M. Alice Smith and Edward Thompson, Dec. 4, 1723.
B. John, son of John and Sarah Smith, Aug. 14, 1725.
M. John Smith and Pleasant Rose, Sept. 30, 1725.
D. Matthew Smith, Dec. 10, 1725.
M. Elizabeth Smith and Edward McDonald, Feb. 6, 1725/6.
M. John Smith and Margaret Grigsby, Nov. 5, 1728.
D. Margaret Smith, Aug. 17, 1728.
M. Henry Smith and Margaret Spicer, Sept. 23, 1729.
M. Sarah Smith and John-Ben Gregg, June 22, 1730.
M. Elizabeth Smith and John White, Nov. 12, 1730.
B. Anne, dau. of John and Margaret Smith, Sept. 2, 1731.
B. Mary, dau. of Henry and Margaret Smith, July 15, 1732.
D. Margaret Smith, Apr. 13, 1733.
M. Henry Smith and Jane Kelly, Sept. 24, 1733.
B. Edward, son of Henry and Jane Smith, June 20, 1734.
D. Mary, dau. of Henry and Margaret Smith, Nov. 15, 1734.
B. Charles, son of John and Margaret Smith, Sept. 20, 1735.
D. Peter Smith, Dec. 28, 1735.
M. Elizabeth Smith and Edward McDonald, Feb. 6, 1735/6.
D. Sarah Smith, May 24, 1736.
D. John, son of John Smith, June 26, 1736.
B. John, son of Henry and Jane Smith, Apr. 7, 1737.
B. Sarah, dau. of John and Margaret Smith, July 14, 1738.
B. Sarah, dau. of Henry and Jane Smith, Feb. 10, 1739/40.
B. John, son of John and Margaret Smith, Oct. 3, 1740.
B. Henry, son of John and Margaret Smith, June 15, 1742.
B. Elizabeth, dau. of Henry and Jane Smith, Aug. 11, 1743.
B. Katherine, dau. of John and Margaret Smith, Nov. 18, 1743.
B. Keziah, dau. of Joseph and Elizabeth Smith, Dec. 21, 1743.
B. Margaret Smith, Apr. 18, 1745.
M. Jemima Smith of Washington Parish and William Monroe, Apr. 2, 1746.
M. Joseph Smith and Mary Shropshire of Hanover Parish, Apr. 3, 1746.
B. John, son of John and Margaret Smith, July 19, 1746.
D. Jane, wife of Henry Smith, Nov. 21, 1748.
M. John Smith and Anne Allenthrope, Mar. 7, 1748/9.
M. Henry Smith and Hester Stone, May 21, 1749.
B. Mildred, dau. of John and Elizabeth Smith, Mar. 22, 1752.
B. William, son of William and Elizabeth Smith, Aug. 13, 1752.
M. Anne Smith and Charles Christie, Mar. 18, 1753.

M. Henry Smith and Elizabeth Jackson, July 11, 1753.
B. John, son of John and Elizabeth Smith, Sept. 27, 1754.
B. Mary, dau. of Henry and Elizabeth Smith, Oct. 13, 1755.
M. Henry Smith, junr: and Sarah Johnson, Mar. 19, 1755.
B. Jane, dau. of Henry and Sarah Smith, Apr. 2, 1756.
B. Charles, son of William and Elizabeth Smith, Dec. 12, 1757.
B. Mildred, dau. of William and Sarah Smith, Apr. 17, 1758.
M. Margaret Smith and John Day, May 15, 1758.
B. Mildred, dau. of Charles and Sarah Smith, Jan. 1, 1759.
M. Charles Smith and Sarah Gregg, Jan. 20, 1759.
B. Winifred, dau. of Henry and Elizabeth Smith, Nov. 20, 1759.
M. Elizabeth Smith and Richard McLachlan, Jan. 31, 1760.
B. Catherine, dau. of George and Behethland Smith, Mar. 24, 1760.
B. Jacob, son of Henry and Sarah Smith, Dec. 3, 1760.
B. Margaret, dau. of Charles and Sarah Smith, Mar. 4, 1761.
B. Mary, dau. of John and Elizabeth Smith, May 13, 1761.
B. Sarah, dau. of George Smith, Mar. 1, 1762.
B. Charles, son of Charles and Sarah Smith, May 27, 1764.
B. Winifred, dau. of Charles and Sarah Smith, Dec. 10, 1765. (?)
M. John Smith and Anne Balb (Ball?), Dec. 26, 1765.
B. Margaret, dau. of John and Anne Smith, Nov. 20, 1766.
M. Henry Smith and Sarah Leech, Dec. 29, 1767.
M. Elizabeth Smith and William Lewis Murphy, Apr. 5, 1768.
M. Charles Smith and Anne Griggs, Jan. 24, 1769.
B. Letitia, dau. of Charles and Anne Smith, July 15, 1771.
B. Behethland, dau. of George and Behethland Smith, Apr. 16, 1772.
B. Margaret, dau. of Charles and Anne Smith, Feb. 9, 1772.
B. Sarah, dau. of Henry and Sarah Smith, June 12, 1774.
M. Mildred Smith and Thomas Brown, Dec. 16, 1773.
M. John Smith and Mary Stribling, Jan. 8, 1778.
M. Henry Smith and Anne Gutridge, July 17, 1778.
M. Jacob Smith and Anne Johnson, Nov. 1, 1781.
M. Nathan Smith and Betsy Washington, Apr. 4, 1790.
M. William Smoot and Frances Bunbury, Sept. 23, 1775.
M. Thomas South and Dorothy Buckley, July 10, 1753.
B. William, son of Thomas and Dorothy South, Aug. 3, 1754.
M. Molly Sparkes and John Henneage, Oct. 22, 1785.
M. Lettice Speerman of Washington Parish and John Douling, May 1, 1746.
M. Elizabeth Spicer (Spiller?) and William Bruton, June 5, 1725.
M. Sarah Spicer and William Burton, Dec. 14, 1725.
M. Rachel Spicer and Isaac Sebastian, May 11, 1727.
M. Margaret Spicer and Henry Smith, Sept. 23, 1729.
B. William, son of William and Elizabeth Spicer, Apr. 6, 1732.
M. Anne Spiecer of this Parish and John Clanton of Hanover Parish, Feb. 17, 1731/2.
B. Lettice, dau. of William and Margaret Spicer, Jan. 20, 1733/4.
M. Benjamin Spicer and Rose Grigsby, June 6, 1734.
M. Joseph Spicer and Margaret Swillivan, Sept. 14, 1741.
M. George Spicer and Sarah Skidmore, July 1, 1744.
M. Lettice Spicer and Francis Fletcher, Nov. 8, 1745.
D. George Spiller, May 21, 1718.
M. William Spillman and Mildred Duling, Dec. 22, 1787.
M. John Spinks of Brunswick Parish and Rosamond Corbin of this Parish, Nov. 6, 1741.[61]
B. Elizabeth, dau. of John and Rosamond Spinks, Aug. 28, 1745.
B. Mary Stanford's son William, Nov. 3, 1720.

D. William, son of Mary Stanford, Nov. 10, 1721.
M. James Staples and Jane Owens, Feb. 12, 1778.
M. William Staples and Frances Paulet, Feb. 18, 1790.
M. Anne Steed and John Story, Feb. 18, 1759.
M. William Steele and Anne Prestridge, Apr. 27, 1742.
M. John Stephens and Mary Whiting, Feb. 24, 1725/6.
B. John, son of John and Elizabeth Stephens, Dec. 5, 1726.
M. James Stevens and Margaret Elkins, June 21, 1727.
M. William Stevenson and Mary Collins, Sept. 24, 1761.
M. Mary Stewart and William Scapelan, Feb. 21, 1754.
M. Catherine Stigler and Robert Stringfellow, May 15, 1762.
M. Elizabeth Stith and Henry Fitzhugh, Oct. 28, 1770.
M. Buckner Stith and Anne Dade, Feb. 26, 1772.
B. Baldwin Buckner, son of Buckner Stith and Anne, his wife, Feb. 3, 1773.
M. Robert Stith and Mary Townshend Washington, July 29, 1773.
M. John Stith and Anne Washington, Dec. 11, 1783.
M. Griffin Stith and Frances Townshend Washington, June 14, 1788.
M. George Stone and Catherine Schofield, July 1, 1715.
D. Catherine Stone, January 25, 1725/6.
M. George Stone and Mary Toul, June 4, 1726.
D. Mary, wife of George Stone, Jan. 10, 1726/7.
D. George Stone, Mar. 12, 1726/7.
M. John Stone and Martha Davies, May 16, 1739.
B. Mary, dau. of John and Martha Stone, Apr. 30, 1740.
M. Eli Stone and Rebecca Davis, Dec. 4, 1746.
B. John, son of Eli and Rebecca Stone, Nov. 18, 1748.
M. Hester Stone and Henry Smith, May 21, 1749.
M. Josias Stone and Margaret Cash, Apr. 8, 1780.[62]
D. John, son of William and Elizabeth (Storke?), Aug. 21, 1716.
B. Behethland, dau. of Wm. and Elizabeth Storke, Dec. 27, 1716, and baptized
    Feb. 17, 1716/7.
B. Margaret, dau. of Wm. and Elizabeth Storke, Jan. 18, 1720/1.
B. Catherine, dau. of William and Elizabeth Storke, Dec. 17, 1723.
B. John, son of William and Elizabeth Storke, July 11, 1725 and baptized Aug.
    15.
M. Elizabeth Storke and Richard Bernard, Aug. 29, 1729.[63]
B. Behethland Storke of this Parish and Anthony Strother of St. George Parish,
    Aug. 25, 1733.
M. Margaret Storke and John Washington, Nov. 23, 1738.
M. Elizabeth Storke and Henry Washington, Junr: May 18, 1743.
M. Catherine Storke and Bailey Washington, Jan. 12, 1748/9.
M. John Storke and Frances Hooe, Mar. 21, 1750/1.[64]
B. William, son of John and Frances Storke, Sept. 25, 1753 and baptized
    Nov. 1.
M. John Story and Anne Steed, Feb. 18, 1759.
D. Hugh Strahan, Apr. 11, 1745.
B. Clarinda, dau. of William and Sarah Strange, Mar. 1, 1766.
M. Sarah Stransford and Anthony Lucas, Nov. 4, 1737.
M. Benoni Stratton and Anne Derrick, Dec. 24, 1733.
B. Frances, dau. of Benoni and Anne Stratton, Oct. 28, 1734.
B. Thomas Derrick, son of Benoni and Anne Stratton, Nov. 3, 1736.
B. Katherine, dau. of Benoni and Anne Stratton, Feb. 13, 1738/9.
B. Susanna, dau. of Benoni Stratton, Mar. 5, 1740/1.
B. William, son of Benoni Stratton, Apr. 20, 1742.
B. Benoni, son of Benoni Stratton, Aug. 22, 1744.
M. Anne Stratton and John Edison (Addison?), July 12, 1751.

M. Frances Stratton and William Lord, Oct. 31, 1756.
M. Benoni Stratton and Elizabeth Lewis, Sept. 29, 1772.
M. Margaret, dau. of Benjamin Stribling, Jan. 11, 1716/5. (sic)
D. Margaret, dau. of Benjamin Stribling, Jan. 12, 1715/6.
M. Thomas Stribling and Elizabeth Newton, Dec. 7, 1725.
B. Newton, son of Thomas and Elizabeth Stribling, Nov. 11, 1726.
B. Thomas, son of Thomas and Elizabeth Stribling, Apr. 20, 1728.
D. Elizabeth Stribling, May 12, 1728.
M. Sarah Stribling and Peter Kerr, Aug. 23, 1728.
M. Thomas Stribling and Jane Thomas, Nov. 17, 1729.
B. John, son of Thomas and Jane (Stribling?), ...1730.
B. William, son of Thomas and Jane Stribling, Jan. 20, 1730/1.
B. Frances, dau. of Thomas and Jane Stribling, June 20, 1734.
B. Jane, dau. of Thomas and Jane Stribling, Jan. 21, 1736/7.
M. Anne Stribling of this Parish and Bushrod Doggett of Brunswick Parish,
       Oct. 6, 1737.
B. Elizabeth, dau. of Thomas and Jane Stribling, Sept.18, 1739.
B. Anne, dau. of Thomas and Jane Stribling, Jan. 18, 1741/2.
D. Benjamin Stribling, Feb. 10, 1742/3.
B. Margaret, dau. of Thomas and Jane Stribling, Mar. 10, 1743/4.
B. Millie (Mildred?), dau. of Thos. and Jane Stribling, Jan. 28, 1747/8.
B. Mary, dau. of Thomas and Jane Stribling, Sept. 17, 1759.
M. Thomas Stribling and Elizabeth Peck, Mar. 8, 1752.
B. Newton, son of Thomas and Elizabeth Stribling, Oct. 10, 1752.
M. William Stribling and Elizabeth Derrick, Jan. 7, 1753.
B. Sarah, dau. of Thomas and Jane Stribling, May 17, 1753.
B. Jemima, dau. of William and Elizabeth Stribling, Mar. 26, 1754.
B. William, son of William and Elizabeth Stribling, Mar. 28, 1755.
B. Joel, son of Thomas and Jane Stribling, Aug. 17, 1756.
B. Winifred, dau. of Wm. and Elizabeth Stribling, July 20, 1757.
M. Jane Stribling and John Curry, Sept. 20, 1758.
B. William Derrick, son of Wm. and Elizabeth Stribling, June 12, 1759.
B. Thomas, son of William and Elizabeth Stribling, Feb. 9, 1761.
B. Jemima, dau. of Wm. and Elizabeth Stribling, Jan. 29, 1764.
M. Margaret Stribling and Reuben Burgess, Sept. 1, 1765.
M. Elizabeth Stribling and Anthony Price, Jan. 17, 1768.
M. Mildred Stribling and John Knowling, Apr. 11, 1776.
M. Margaret Stribling and James Rawlings, Jan. 5, 1778.
M. Mary Stribling and John Smith, Jan. 8, 1778.
B. Lucy, dau. of James and Susanna Stringfellow, Jan. 11, 1761.
M. Robert Stringfellow and Catherine Stigler, May 15, 1762.
B. Elizabeth, dau. of Robert and Catherine Stringfellow, Jan. 29, 1768.
B. Benjamin and Anne, son and dau. of Joel and Mary Stripling, May 31,
       1715.[65]
D. Joel Stripling, Sept. 14, 1718.
M. Joel Stripling and Hester Colclough, Sept. 25, 1723.
B. Colclough, son of Joel and Hester Stripling, ...1728.
B. Hester, dau. of Joel and Hester Stripling, Apr. 5, 1732.
B. Bradford, son of Joel and Hester Stripling, Jan. 11, 1735/6.
D. Joel Stripling, Mar. 19, 1737/8.
B. Mary, dau. of Joel and Hester Stripling, Nov. 4, 1738.
M. Hester Stripling and Thomas Lewis Barrett, Apr. 16, 1744.
D. Joel, son of Joel and Hester Stripling, Sept. 27, 1744.
M. Colclough Stripling and Mary Hodge, Oct. 6, 1749.
B. Joel, son of Colclough and Frances Stripling, Mar. 11, 1753.
M. Hester Stripling and Francis Rose, May 31, 1756.

B. Benjamin, son of Colclough and Frances Stripling, June 15, 1756.
B. Joel, son of Colclough and Frances Stripling, Mar. 8, 1758.
B. John Colclough, son of Colclough and Frances Stripling, Jan. 5, 1760.
B. Susanna, dau. of Colclough and Frances Stripling, Apr. 27, 1764.
B. Thomas, son of Colclough and Frances Stripling, Oct. 22, 1766.
B. Mary, dau. of Colclough and Frances Stripling, Feb. 16, 1769.
M. Alice Strother of Overwharton Parish and Robert Washington of this Parish, Dec. 16, 1756.
M. Anthony Strother of St. George's Parish and Behethland Storke of this Parish, Aug. 25, 1733.
M. Elizabeth Strother and Robert Key, Dec. 13, 1762.
M. Enoch Strother and Mary Key, Feb. 12, 1763.
M. Anne Strother and John James, Sept. 16, 1763.
M. William Strother and Winifred Baker of Westmoreland, Sept. 26, 1765.
B. William, son of the Rev. David and Jane Stuart, Dec. 13, 1723.
M. James Stuart and Margaret Reiney, Mar. 24, 1724/5.
B. Mary, dau. of the Rev. David and Jane Stuart, Feb. 24, 1725/6.
B. John, son of the Rev. David and Jane Stuart, May 10, 1728.
B. Sarah, dau. of the Rev. David and Jane Stuart, Feb. 21, 1730/1.
B. Charles, son of the Rev. David and Jane Stuart, Apr. 16, 1733.
B. Frances, dau. of Joseph and Sarah Stuart, Nov. 1, 1735.
M. Alexander Stuart and Mary Turner, Dec. 23, 1739.
B. Margaret, dau. of Alexander and Mary Stuart, Apr. 17, 1742.
M. Mary Stuart and Sigismund Massey, Apr. 4, 1743.
D. Alexander Stuart, Jan. 24, 1742/3.
M. Mary Stuart and James Boswell, Apr. 6, 1744.
D. The Rev. David Stuart, Rector S. P., Jan. 31, 1748/9.
D. Mrs. Jane Stuart, Relict of ye Revd David Stuart, Jan. 24, 1749/50.
M. John Stuart and Frances Alexander, Feb. 16, 1749/50.
M. Sarah Stuart and Thomas Fitzhugh, June 19, 1750.
B. William Gibbons, son of John and Frances Stuart, Nov. 25, 1750.
M. William Stuart and Sarah Foote, Nov. 26, 1750.
B. Jane, dau. of William and Sarah Stuart, Dec. 1, 1751.
B. Philip, son of John and Frances Stuart, Feb. 18, 1752.
M. Charles Stuart, and Frances Washington, Feb. 23, 1752.
M. Charles Stuart of King George county and Susanna Grigsby, Nov. 9, 1752.
B. David, son of William and Sarah Stuart, Aug. 3, 1753.
B. John, son of Charles and Frances Stuart, Sept. 22, 1753.
M. Charles Stuart and Frances Dade, Aug. 6, 1754.
B. Martha, dau. of John and Frances Stuart, Oct. 19, 1754.
B. John, son of John and Frances Stuart, Mar. 1, 1757.
B. John Alexander, son of John and Frances Stuart, Apr. 20, 1758.
B. Elizabeth, dau. of Charles and Frances Stuart, Nov. 15, 1758.
B. Mary, dau. of Charles and Frances Stuart, Dec. 22, 1760.
B. Philip, son of John and Frances Stuart, Feb. 22, 1761.
B. William, son of William and Sarah Stuart, Oct. 21, 1761.
B. Henry Foote, son of William and Sarah Stuart, Apr. 25, 1763.
B. Charles, son of John and Frances Stuart, Aug. 23, 1763.
B. Richard, son of William and Sarah Stuart, Sept. 4, 1769.
M. Jane Stuart and Townshend Dade, Dec. 11, 1769.
B. Henry Foote, son of William and Sarah Stuart, Oct. 18, 1772.
M. Martha Stuart and William Thornton, May 11, 1775.
B. Jane, dau. of William and Sarah Stuart, May 15, 1776.
M. Price Stuart and Anne Clifton, Oct. 17, 1781.
M. Charles Stuart and Helen Wray, Oct. 31, 1783.
M. John Alexander Stuart and Mary Wray, Nov. 17, 1785.

D. Henry F., son of the Rev. William Stuart and Sarah, his wife, June 8, 1793.
M. Anne Stuart and William Mason, July 11, 1793.
M. Jane Stuart and Richard Foote, Dec. 16, 1795.
D. William Stuart (Rev.), Oct. 1, 1798, aged 75 years.
M. Elizabeth Sublinel and John Harges, Oct. 1, 1725.
M. John Sudduth and Frances Carver, June 8, 1733.
M. Joseph Sudduth and Margaret Sebastian, Oct. 13, 1735.
B. John, son of John and Frances Sudduth, Apr. 21, 1736.
M. Rose Sudduth and John Kennedy, June 21, 1736.
B. Lettice, dau. of John and Frances Sudduth, July 6, 1738.
B. Mary, dau. of John and Frances Sudduth, Aug. 21, 1740.
D. Margaret, wife of Joseph Sudduth, Nov. 3, 1741.
M. Robert Sudduth, Junr: and Sarah Walker, Jan. 26, 1741/2.
M. Sarah Sudduth and James Grigsby, May 19, 1742.
B. Joseph, son of Robert and Sarah Sudduth, Nov. 2, 1742.
B. Joseph, son of John and Frances Sudduth, Nov. 8, 1742.
B. William, son of John and Frances Sudduth, Mar. 9, 1744/5.
B. Elizabeth, dau. of John and Frances Sudduth, Mar. 14, 1745/6.
B. Mary, dau. of Robert and Sarah Sudduth, Jan. 16, 1746/7.
B. Sarah, dau. of Robert and Sarah Sudduth, Sept. 7, 1748.
M. Hannah Sudduth and John Hall, Nov. 6, 1749.
M. Absolom Sudduth and Sarah Elliott, Oct. 2, 1750.
M. Robert Sudduth and Elizabeth Cooper, Oct. 2, 1750.
M. Joseph Sudduth and Jemima Skidmore, Aug. 18, 1751.[66]
M. Benjamin Sudduth and Mary Sebastian, Feb. 24, 1752.
B. Benjamin, son of Benjamin and Mary Sudduth, Mar. 2, 1757.
B. Isaac, son of Benjamin and Margaret Sudduth, July 6, 1760.
B. William, son of Robert and Sarah Sudduth, Aug. 5, 1764.
M. Lettice Sudduth and John Culham, Feb. 17, 1775.
M. Elinor Sullivan and Hugh McCarty, Apr. 22, 1730.
M. Burgess Sullivan and Anne Carver, Feb. 3, 1747/8.
B. Sallie, dau. of Burgess and Anne Sullivan, Oct. 24, 1748.
B. William, son of Burgess and Anne Sullivan, Oct. 8, 1750.
B. Harry, son of Burgess and Anne Sullivan, July 6, 1758.
M. Mildred Sullivan and William Oakley, Feb. 4, 1781.
M. John Sullivan and Adah Skinner, Apr. 17, 1788.
M. Michael Summers and Hannah Edwards, May 12, 1724.
B. Mary, dau. of Michael and Hannah Summers, Apr. 16, 1728.
B. John and Jemima, son and dau. of Michael and Hannah Summers, July 16, 1732.
B. Sarah, dau. of Michael and Hannah Summers, July 20, 1735.
B. Margaret, dau. of Michael and Hannah Summers, June 14, 1738.
B. Elizabeth, dau. of Michael and Susanna Summers, Dec. 5, 1740.
M. Lettice Summers and James Hansbury, Sept. 19, 1741.
B. Anne, dau. of Michael and Susanna Summers, June 22, 1744.
B. Samuel, son of Michael and Susanna Summers, Nov. 1, 1746.
B. Susanna, dau. of Michael and Hannah (?) Summers, July 25, 1748.
M. Margaret Sumner of Overwharton Parish and John Minor of Brunswick Parish, Feb. 3, 1740/1.
B. Hannah, dau. of Robert and Dinah Suthard, May 2, 1728.[67]
B. Absolom, son of Robert and Diana Suthard, Feb. 21, 1725/6.
B. Moses, son of Robert and Diana Suthard, Sept. 22, 1732.
M. Anne Sutherland and Gustavus Elgin, Mar. 26, 1793.
M. John Sutton and Martha Kenneman, Sept. 17, 1723.
D. Martha Sutton, Dec. 10, 1725.
M. Thomas Sweatman and Frances Call, Dec. 16, 1765.
M. Paul Sweeny and Frances Williams, Dec. 24, 1728.

B. Sarah, dau. of Paul and Frances Sweeny, Oct. 23, 1731.
M. Sarah Sweeny and Peter Culvey, Mar. 28, 1758.
M. Sarah Sweeny and Elias Rose, Sept. 2, 1758.
M. Elizabeth Sweeny and James Jackson, Dec. 31, 1767.
M. John Sweeny and Margaret Addison, Oct. 6, 1769.
M. Frances Sweeny and James Smallwood, May 23, 1776.
M. Susanna Sweeny and William Burke, Feb. 1, 1778.
M. Anne Swillakeen and John Rose, Jan. 4, 1776.
M. Margaret Swillivan and Joseph Spicer, Sept. 14, 1741.

T

D. Robert Taliaferro, June 6, 1726.
M. Richard Taliaferro of Essex and Rose Berryman of King George, June 10, 1726.
M. Frances Taliaferro and Kenelm Cheseldine, Aug. 9, 1768.
M. John Taliaferro and Lucy Alexander, Jan. 24, 1774.
M. Lawrence Taliaferro and Sarah Dade, Feb. 3, 1774.
M. Margaret Tamian and William Ward, Dec. 24, 1741.
M. George Tavernor and Elizabeth Bishop, Jan. 2, 1739/40.
B. John, son of John and Anne Taylor, Aug. 20, 1718.
M. John Taylor and Mary Moss, Aug. 19, 1724.
D. Mary Taylor, Mar. 25, 1726.
M. John Taylor and Mary Ancrum, Feb. 27, 1726/7.
B. William, son of John and Mary Taylor, Mar. 23, 1727/8.
D. Mary Taylor, Oct. 21, 1732.
M. John Taylor and Verlinda Dunahoo, Dec. 13, 1776.
M. Sarah Taylor and Zachariah Rose, Mar. 19, 1778.
M. Mary Taylor and Reuben Settle, July 15, 1792.
M. Daniel Taylour and Sarah Carver, Jan. 19, 1764.
B. Jane, dau. of Edward and Sarah Templeman, Dec. 7, 1747.
B. Mary, dau. of Henry and Susanna Tennyson, Apr. 7, 1718.
D. Mary, dau. of Henry and Susanna Tennyson, Sept. 11, 1718.
B. Mary, dau. of Henry and Susanna Tennyson, Aug. 9, 1719 (?).
D. Susanna Tennyson, Apr. 4, 1720.
B. Richard, son of Daniel and Anne Ternan, Nov. 25, 1745.
B. John, son of Richard and Sarah Tho(mas), Nov. 10, 1717.
M. William Thomas and Thomison Hamm, Dec. 22, 1724.
D. William Thomas, June 2, 1725.
B. Anne, dau. of William and Thomison Thomas, Nov. 5, 1725.
M. Mary Thomas and John Ancrum, Jan. 27, 1726/7.
B. Verlinda, dau. of William and Thomison Thomas, Apr. 20, 1728.
M. Jane Thomas and Thomas Stribling, Nov. 17, 1729.
M. Massey Thomas and Mary Price, Nov. 28, 1731.
B. John, son of Massey and Mary Thomas, Apr. 26, 1732.
B. Anne, dau. of William and Thomison Thomas, Dec. 12, 1733.
B. William, son of Massey and Mary Thomas, Oct. 12, 1734.
B. Sarah, dau. of Massey and Sarah Thomas, Sept. 28, 1737.
B. George, son of Massey and Mary Thomas, Feb. 28, 1738/9.
B. Milly, dau. of William and Thomison Thomas, Dec. 15, 1739.
B. Anne, dau. of Massey and Mary Thomas, Mar. 15, 1740/1.
M. John Thomas and Jemima Derrick, Aug. 10, 1741.
B. Sarah, dau. of John and Jemima Thomas, Apr. 10, 1742.
B. Mary, dau. of John and Jemima Thomas, May 26, 1744.
B. William, son of John and Jemima Thomas, Nov. 16, 1746.
D. Richard Thomas, Dec. 3, 1748.

M. Sarah Thomas and Lovel White, Dec. 14, 1749.
B. Jane, dau. of John and Jemima Thomas, July 19, 1750.
M. William Thomas and Jane Johnson, Dec. 25, 1752.
B. Susanna, dau. of William and Sarah Thomas, Feb. 3, 1755.
M. Anthony Buckner Thomas and Amy Powell, Apr. 20, 1755.
B. Elizabeth, dau. of William and Sarah Thomas, Oct. 7, 1757.
M. Sarah Thomas and John Gray, May 11, 1758.
M. John Thomas and Mary Thomas, Feb. 19, 1762.
M. Jane Thomas and Thomas King, May 19, 1771.
M. Price Thomas and Mary Monroe, Nov. 7, 1779.
M. Mary Thomas and Aaron Mardus, Mar. 12, 1785.
M. William Thomas and Mary White, Dec. 13, 1785.
D. Ruth, dau. of Elizabeth Thompson, May 18, 1718.
M. Edward Thomson and Alice Smith, Dec. 4, 1723.
D. William Thompson, Dec. 30, 1725.
M. William Thompson and Jane Holland, Dec. 26, 1765.
B. James, son of William and Jane Thompson, Feb. 24, 1768.
B. Sarah, dau. of William and Sarah (Jane?) Thompson, Aug. 5, 1769.
B. William, son of William and Sarah (Jane?) Thompson, June 14, 1772.
B. Jane, dau. of William and Jane Thompson, Sept. 29, 1774.
M. Margaret Thompson and William Christie, June 6, 1775.
M. Sarah Thompson and Dennis Mehorner, Feb. 21, 1781.
M. William Thompson and Anne Washington, Aug. 3, 1785.
M. Andrew Thompson and Mary Rose, Jan. 2, 1787.
M. Richard Thomison and Elizabeth Oxford, June 3, 1724.
M. James Thomson and Elizabeth Armour, Aug. 10, 1724.
B. James, son of James and Elizabeth Thomson, Nov. 15, 1726.
M. Elizabeth Thomson and John Selvie, June 29, 1727.
D. Edward Thomson, Sept. 24, 1728.
D. Richard Thornberry, Sept. 11, 1716.
M. Mary Thornberry of St. Paul's Parish and William Horton of King George
   county, Jan. 12, 1741/2.
M. Samuel Thornberry and Mary Kidwell, Apr. 20, 1744.
B. John Kidwell, son of Samuel and Mary Thornberry, Feb. 19, 1744/5.
B. Elizabeth, dau. of Samuel and Mary Thornberry, Apr. 15, 1746.
B. William, son of William and Elizabeth Thornberry, Mar. 20, 1748/9.[68]
M. John Thornberry and Elizabeth Bolling, Dec. 14, 1749.
B. Henry, son of John and Elizabeth Thornberry, July 12, 1750.
B. John, son of John and Elizabeth Thornberry, Jan. 3, 1752.
B. Peggy, dau. of John and Elizabeth Thornberry, Oct. 5, 1753.
B. John Deneal, son of Wm. and Elizabeth Thornberry, Dec. 4, 1753.
B. Mary, dau. of John and Elizabeth Thornberry, Nov. 4, 1757.
B. William, son of John and Elizabeth Thornberry, Oct. 10, 1760.
B. Francis, son of Anthony and Winifred Thornton, July 20, 1725.
B. Anthony, son of Anthony and Winifred Thornton, Nov. 15, 1727.
M. Elizabeth Thornton and John Ford, Jan. 27, 1729/30.
B. Judith Presley, dau. of Anthony and Winifred Thornton, Oct. 3, 1731.
D. Judith Presley, dau. of Captain Anthony and Winifred Thornton, Oct. 11,
   1733.
B. Peter, son of Anthony and Winifred Thornton, Mar. 29, 1734.
M. Francis Thornton and Sarah Fitzhugh, Apr. 2, 1747.
B. Winifred, dau. of Anthony (?) and Sarah Thornton, Jan. 14, 1747/8.
M. Winifred Thornton and William Bernard, Nov. 25, 1750.
B. Sarah, dau. of Francis and Sarah Thornton, Feb. 10, 1752.
M. William Thornton and Elizabeth Fitzhugh, Apr. 26, 1757.
B. Susanna, dau. of William and Susanna (Elizabeth?) Thornton, Mar. 29, 1758.

B. William, son of Francis and Sarah Thornton, May 28, 1758.
M. John Thornton and Behethland Gilson Berryman, Dec. 13, 1761.
M. Anthony Thornton and Susanna Fitzhugh, Jan. 5, 1764.
M. Winifred Thornton and Daniel McCarty, Jan. 15, 1765.
M. George Thornton and Mary Alexander, Oct. 9, 1773.
M. William Thornton and Martha Stuart, May 11, 1775.
M. Lucy Thornton and John Brooke, July 2, 1777.
M. Elizabeth Thornton and Presley Thornton, Mar. 26, 1784.
M. Presley Thornton and Elizabeth Thornton, Mar. 26, 1784.
M. Alice Thornton and Presley Thornton, Oct. 19, 1785.
M. Presley Thornton and Alice Thornton, Oct. 19, 1785.
M. Elizabeth Ticlcock and James Hartley, Apr. 1, 1768.
M. Thomas Timmons and Susanna Owens, May 14, 1749.
M. Mary Todd and John Murray, Dec. 12, 1727.
B. William, son of Richard and Lucy Todd, Feb. 12, 1727/8.
D. Richard Todd, Jan. 18, 1736/7.[69]
M. Lucy Todd and John Martin, Nov. 5, 1742.
B. Samuel, son of Hayward and Sarah Todd, July 28, 1747.
B. Hester, dau. of Hayward and Mary (Sarah?) Todd, Apr. 13, 1750.
B. Lucy, dau. of Hayward and Sarah Todd, Mar. 27, 1751.
M. James Tolmark and Mary Clark, May 17, 1792.
M. William Toul and Mary Porter, Oct. 15, 1722.
M. Mary Toul and George Stone, June 4, 1726.
M. Elizabeth Townley and Richard Moody, Feb. 5, 1758.
M. John Tracy of Washington Parish and Anne Caplee, Aug. 7, 1740.
B. Luke, son of John and Anne Tracy, Mar. 14, 1740/1.
B. James, son of John and Anne Tracy, Feb. 12, 1744/5.
M. Letitia Travers and James Grigsby, Jan. 18, 1753.
B. Lucy, dau. of William and Margaret Travers, Dec. 13, 1762.
M. John Travis and Margaret Hubert, June 28, 1722.
B. John, son of John and Anne Trayle, Dec. 13, 1742.
M. Anne Tregar and William Crismund, Apr. 28, 1779.
M. Mary Trenar and Joseph Cooke, Dec. 26, 1723.
B. Anne, dau. of Mary Trigger, Jan. 11, 1732/3.
M. Mary Trigger and William King, Aug. 2, 1735.
M. William Trigger and Sarah Levy, Feb. 1, 1786.
M. Mary Triplett and George Hibbill (?Hill), Feb. 12, 1728/9.
B. William, son of Thomas and Katherine Trott, Nov. 5, 1742.
B. Francis, son of Francis and Susannah Triplett, Feb. 12, 1732/3.
M. Benjamin Truslow and Keziah Mannard, Mar. 12, 1786.
M. Thomas Truslow and Zilpah Skinner, Jan. 19, 1789.
M. Joseph Tucker and Rosamond Carroll of Brunswick Parish, Feb. 20, 1733/4.[70]
M. John Tunnell and Sarah Martin, Feb. 18, 1763.
M. Mildred Tunnell and Woodford Kelly, Feb. 4, 1769.
M. John Tunnell and Elizabeth Long, Feb. 13, 1774.
M. Elizabeth Tunnel and William Sacheverel, Feb. 26, 1784.
M. Richard Turner and Helena Carter, Sept. 24, 1725.
D. Eleanor (Helena?) Turner, Oct. 11, 1739.
M. Mary Turner and Alexander Stuart, Dec. 23, 1739.
M. John Turner and Sarah Derrick, Oct. 2, 1741.
B. William, son of John and Sarah Turner, Aug. 24, 1742.
B. John, son of John and Anne (Sarah?) Turner, Oct. 28, 1744.
B. Joseph, son of John and Sarah Turner, Apr. 16, 1747.
M. Sarah Turner and John Norris, Aug. 29, 1751.
B. John, son of John and Sarah Turner, Aug. 29, 1767.
M. John Turner and Martha Derrick, Sept. 2, 1769.

B. William, son of John and Martha Turner, Apr. 9, 1771.
B. Sarah, dau. of John and Martha Turner, Sept. 6, 1772.
B. John Mattox, son of John and Martha Turner, Dec. 16, 1774.
M. Thomas Tyler and Elizabeth Settle, Jan. 5, 1787.

U

M. Fanny Underwood and John Lee, Mar. 2, 1790.

V

M. William Vaint and Catherine Reddish, Aug. 27, 1723.
B. Sarah, dau. of William and Catherine Vaint, July 3, 1725.
M. Richard Vincent and Grace Cheesman, Dec. 31, 1730.[71]
B. Cornelius, son of Richard and Grace Vincent, Oct. 14, 1731.
B. Jane, dau. of Richard and Jane (Grace?) Vincent, June 23, 1733.
M. Jane Vincent and George Gregg, Feb. 5, 1734/5.
M. Richard Vincent and Elizabeth Gregg, Apr. 29, 1737.
B. William, son of Richard and Elizabeth Vincent, Nov. 27, 1738.
D. Elizabeth, wife of Richard Vincent, Dec. 2, 1738.
D. Richard Vincent, July 23, 1741.
M. Thomas Vincent and Elizabeth Pennuel, Apr. 3, 1749.
B. George, son of James and Elizabeth Vincent, Apr. 10, 1749.
M. Rebecca Vowles and William Berryman, Sept. 10, 1743.

W

M. Sarah Waemark and James Brown, May 11, 1760.
M. Mildred Wagstaff and George Hutcheson, Sept. 19, 1727.
D. Ralph Walker, Apr. 20, 1716.
M. Ralph Walker and Sarah Bussey, Jan. 26, 1722/3.
B. Martha, dau. of Ralph and Sarah Walker, Aug. 15, 1725.
M. Sarah Walker and John Baker, Oct. 30, 1725.
B. Mary, dau. of Richard and Elizabeth Walker, Aug. 25, 1726.
B. Richard, son of Richard and Elizabeth Walker, Apr. 17, 1732.
M. William Walker and Elizabeth Netherington, Nov. 23, 1731.
B. Pelatiah, dau. of Richard and Elizabeth Walker, Feb. 23, 1734/5.
D. Thomas, son of Richard and Elizabeth Walker, Nov. 4, 1735.
D. Elizabeth, wife of Richard Walker, Nov. 6, 1735.
D. Elizabeth Walker, Aug. 25, 1737.
M. Sarah Walker and Robert Sudduth, Jun'r: Jan. 26, 1741/2.
B. William, son of William and Elizabeth Walker, Mar. 25, 1744.
B. John, son of William and Elizabeth Walker, May 22, 1745.
B. James, son of William and Elizabeth Walker, Oct. 16, 1746.
B. Elizabeth, dau. of William and Elizabeth Walker, Dec. 22, 1747.
M. Elizabeth Walker and James McCant, Mar. 15, 1747/8.
B. William, son of Richard and Eleanor Walker, Mar. 15, 1749/50.
M. Mary Walker and John Hallett, Aug. 1, 1751.
B. Jane, dau. of Eleanor Walker, July 28, 1756.
M. Mary Walker and James McDuff, Mar. 3, 1757.
M. Anne Walpole and James Hartley, Aug. 26, 1788.
M. Lurena Ward of this Parish and Henry Mintoe of Overwharton Parish, Jan. 16, 1737/8.
M. William Ward and Margaret Tamian, Dec. 24, 1741.
B. Mary, dau. of William and Margaret Ward, Sept. 30, 1742.
D. Margaret, wife of William Ward, Dec. 11, 1742.

B. Henry, son of Mary Ward, Dec. 5, 1747.
B. Peggy, dau. of Mary Ward, Feb. 19, 1750/1.
B. Sarah, dau. of Mary Ward, Sept. 19, 1753.
M. William Ward and Elizabeth Jordan, Dec. 25, 1753.
M. Henry Ward and Mary Rankins, June 14, 1775.
M. James Ward and Anne Willis, June 29, 1777.
B. Edward, son of Alexander and Alice Ware, Mar. 20, 1716/7.
D. Edward, son of Alexander and Alice Ware, Aug. 9, 1717.
D. Alexander Ware, Nov. 5, 1716.
M. Alse (Alice?) Ware and Pemberton Proudlove, Feb. 10, 1717/8.
B. William, son of John and Margaret Warner, Sept. 10, 1725.
D. Mr. Nathaniel Washington, Sept. 15, 1718.
B. Henry, son of John Washington, Apr. 16, 1720.
D. Mary Washington, May 13, 1721.
B. Henry, son of Henry and Mary Washington, ...1721/2.
B. Mildred, dau. of Mr. John Washington, Aug. 3, 1722.[72]
B. Anne, dau. of John and Mary Washington, Nov. 2, 1723.
M. Townshend Washington and Elizabeth Lund, Dec. 22, 1726.
B. Nathaniel, son of Henry and Mary Washington, Jan. 16, 1725/6.
B. Mary, dau. of John and Mary Washington, Feb. 28, 1725/6.
B. Susanna, dau. of Townshend and Elizabeth Washington, Nov. 3, 1727.
B. Lawrence, son of John and Mary Washington, Mar. 31, 1728.
B. Mary, dau. of Henry and Mary (Washington), Aug. 9, 1728.
B. Robert, son of Townshend and Elizabeth Washington, June 25, 1729.
B. John (?), son of Henry and Mary Washington (?), Jan. 22, 1729/30.
B. _____, ___ of John and Mary (?) Washington, Mar. 4, 1729/30.
D. Mrs. Mary Washington, Apr. 1, 1729.
B. Bailey, son of Henry and Mary Washington, Sept. 10, 1731.
B. Thomas, son of Townshend and Elizabeth Washington, Mar. 24, 1730/1.
B. Frances, dau. of John and Mary Washington, Oct. 20, 1731.
B. Townshend, son of Townshend and Elizabeth Washington, Sept. 21, 1733.
B. John, son of John and Mary Washington, Aug. 10, 1734.
D. Mary, wife of Mr. Henry Washington, Jan. 19, 1734/5.
D. John, son of John and Mary Washington, Feb. 13, 1735/6.
B. Townshend, son of Townshend and Elizabeth Washington, Feb. 25, 1735/6.
B. Lund, son of Townshend and Elizabeth Washington, Oct. 21, 1737.
B. Elizabeth, dau. of Capt. John and Mary Washington, Dec. 21, 1737.
M. John Washington and Margaret Storke, Nov. 23, 1738.
B. John and Lawrence, sons of Townshend and Elizabeth Washington, Mar. 14, 1739/40.
B. Catherine, dau. of Capt. John and Mary Washington, Jan. 13, 1740/1.
D. Captain John Washington, Feb. 27, 1741/2.
B. Henry, son of Townshend and Elizabeth Washington, Aug. 29, 1742.
B. Sarah, dau. of Capt. John and Mary Washington, Oct. 28, 1742.
M. Mildred Washington and Langhorne Dade, Feb. 14, 1742/3.
M. Henry Washington, Junr: and Elizabeth Storke, May 18, 1743.
D. Mr. Townshend Washington, Dec. 31, 1743.
B. Lawrence, son of Henry and Elizabeth Washington, Feb. 10, 1743/4.
D. Nathaniel, son of Capt. Henry (John?) Washington, Nov. 28, 1745.
D. Mary Washington, Junr: May 11, 1746.
D. Mary, widow of Nathaniel Washington, Oct. 23, 1747.
D. Captain Henry Washington, Oct. 22, 1748.
B. William, son of John and Margaret Washington, Dec. 9, 1748.
M. Bailey Washington and Catherine Storke, Jan. 12, 1748/9.[73]
M. John Washington and Betty Massey, Nov. 17, 1749.
B. Henry, son of Bailey and Catherine Washington, Dec. 5, 1749.

M. Lawrence Washington and Elizabeth Dade, July 31, 1750.
M. Frances Washington and Charles Stuart, Feb. 23, 1752.
B. William, son of Bailey and Catherine Washington, Feb. 28, 1752.[74]
M. Robert Washington of this Parish and Alice Strother of Overwharton Parish, Dec. 16, 1756.
B. George, son of Lawrence and Elizabeth Washington, Jan. 4, 1758.
B. Thomas, son of Robert and Alice Washington, Sept. 5, 1758.
M. Elizabeth Washington and Thomas Berry, Nov. 19, 1758.
M. Catherine Washington and John Washington of King George, Dec. 23, 1759.
M. John Washington of King George and Catherine Washington, Dec. 23, 1759.
B. William Strother, son of Robert and Alice Washington, Apr. 20, 1760.
B. Henry, son of John and Catherine Washington, Oct. 26, 1760.
M. Elizabeth Washington and John Buckner, Dec. 21, 1760.
B. Anne, dau. of Robert and Alice Washington, Nov. 10, 1761.
M. Margaret Washington and Andrew Monroe, Dec. 21, 1761.
B. Nathaniel, son of John and Catherine Washington, Oct. 1, 1762.
B. Townshend, son of Robert and Alice Washington, Feb. 20, 1764.
B. Mary, dau. of John and Catherine Washington, June 17, 1764.
B. Ferdinand, son of Samuel and Anne Washington, July 16, 1767.
B. Frances Townshend, dau. of Lawrence and Elizabeth Washington, Aug. 18, 1767.
B. Lund, son of Robert and Alice Washington, Sept. 25, 1767.
M. Nathaniel Washington and Sarah Hooe, Dec. 17, 1767.
M. Mary Townshend Washington and Robert Stith, July 29, 1773.
M. Lawrence Washington and Catherine Foote, Oct. 5, 1774.
M. Henry Washington and Mildred Pratt, Mar. 12, 1779.
M. Anne Washington and Thomas Hungerford, June 22, 1780.
M. Anne Washington and John Stith, Dec. 11, 1783.
M. Anne Washington and William Thompson, Aug. 3, 1785.
M. Frances Townshend Washington and Thornton Augustine Washington, Apr. 2, 1786.
M. John Washington and Eleanor Massey, Dec. 24, 1787.
M. Frances Townshend Washington and Griffin Stith, June 14, 1788.
M. Betsy Washington and Nathan Smith, Apr. 4, 1790.
M. George Nailour Wassle and Mary Griffith, July 26, 1792.
M. John Watson and Sarah Addison, Feb. 27, 1790.
D. George Watt, Aug. 22, 1730.
M. John Waugh and Jane Massey, Apr. 22, 1761.
M. Gracey Waugh and Elisha Perry, Jan. 30, 1783.
M. John Waugh and Mary Watts Ashton, Nov. 4, 1790.
M. Elizabeth Weedon of Washington Parish and the Rev. Robert McCullock, Feb. 17, 1734/5.
M. John Welch and Mary Hudson, Nov. 16, 1727.
M. Robert Welch and Elizabeth Yates, Aug. 12, 1729.
D. John, son of Samuel Wells, Aug. 10, 1716.
D. Samuel Wells, Sept. 9, 1716.
D. Joseph, brother of William Wells, Dec. 19, 1717.
M. John Wells and Frances Barnfather, June 18, 1723.
M. Samuel Wells and Susanna Brandison, July 8, 1723.
B. Thomas, son of John and Frances Wells, Sept. 17, 1724.
B. Anthony, son of Samuel and Susanna Wells, Feb. 27, 1725/6.
B. John, son of John and Frances Wells, Feb. 12, 1727/8.
B. _____, of Samuel Wells, May 2, 1730.
D. Elinor Wells, Dec. 15, 1729.
B. Charles, son of Samuel and Susanna Wells, May 12, 1731.
M. Charles Wells and Mary Edwards, Dec. 10, 1733.[75]

B. Samuel, son of Charles and Mary Wells, Sept. 16, 1734.
B. James Penney, son of Jeremiah and Elizabeth Wetherly, Dec. 26, 1753.
M. Elizabeth Wharton and Thomas Settle, Feb. 26, 1778.
M. Patty Wharton and William Johnson, Aug. 5, 1778.
M. John Whitcraft and Mary Magdelene Delore (?), Sept. 25, 1716.
M. John White and Elizabeth Smith, Nov. 12, 1730.
M. Behethland White and Samuel Kelly, Aug. 25, 1741.
M. Lovel White and Sarah Thomas, Dec. 14, 1749.
M. Sarah White of King George County and George Arnold, Nov. 9, 1758.
M. Nathan Skipwith White and Mary Burgess, Apr. 15, 1759.
B. Roderick, son of Nathan Skipwith and Mary White, Oct. 3, 1760.
M. Anne White and George Nash, Jan. 20, 1769.
M. Alexander White and Priscilla Flower, Apr. 30, 1775.
M. Mary White and William Thomas, Dec. 13, 1785.
M. John White and Dolly Peed, Jan. 3, 1790.
M. Bartlett White and Elizabeth Mardus, Mar. 2, 1792.
M. Anderson White and Mary Branner, Oct. 14, 1794.
B. Anne, dau. of Isaac and Elizabeth Whiting, Aug. 5, 1715.
B. Mary, dau. of Isaac and Elizabeth Whiting, Apr. 18, 1718.
B. Samuel, son of Isaac and Elizabeth Whiting, Sept. 14, 1723.
D. Sarah Whiting, Jan. 28, 1723/4.
D. Isaac Whiting, Dec. 15, 1725.
M. Mary Whiting and John Stephens, Feb. 24, 1725/6.
B. Anne Whiting, Mar. 25, 1737.
M. Lawrence Whiting and Jane Kelly, Aug. 29, 1744.
B. Richard, son of Samuel and Jane Whiting, Jan. 24, 1744/5.
M. Samuel Whiting and Sarah Hall, Oct. 5, 1750.
M. Maxfield Whiting and Lettice Johnson, Feb. 3, 1753.
B. John, son of Maxfield and Lettice Whiting, Feb. 6, 1755.
M. Martha Whiting and Daniel Fingleston, Feb. 10, 1755.
B. Mary, dau. of John and Mary Whiting, Feb. 10, 1756.
M. Sarah Whiting and Thomas Duncomb, June 2, 1758.
B. Elizabeth, dau. of John and Mary Whiting, Sept. 9, 1758.
B. John, son of Samuel and Sarah Whiting, Jan. 17, 1759.
B. George, son of Maxfield and Lettice Whiting, Dec. 20, 1761.
M. Martha Whiting and Benjamin Derrick, Jan. 31, 1763.
M. Mary Whiting and George Boyle, June 2, 1778.
M. Anne Whiting and John Beattie, Sept. 10, 1779.
M. John Whiting and Nancy Gouldie, Oct. 25, 1785.
M. Sarah Whiting and Lovell Massey, Dec. 28, 1786.
M. John Whiting and Mildred Jones, Dec. 26, 1788.
M. John Whiting and Mary McLean, Aug. 10, 1791.
M. John Whitledge of Hamilton Parish and Elizabeth Overall of this Parish,
      Sept. 15, 1733.
M. Nathaniel Whitledge of Hamilton Parish and Frances Overall of this Parish,
      Oct. 27, 1733.
M. Lydia Whitledge of Hamilton Parish and Thomas Green, Mar. 29, 1746.
M. William Whitmore and Molly Carver, Jan. 5, 1781.
D. Henry Widgeon, Jan. 27, 1725/6.
B. Elizabeth, dau. of John and Anne Wiggins, Mar. 9, 1758.
M. Elizabeth Wiggins and James (?) Rogers, Aug. 12, 1787.
M. Elizabeth Wiggins and Benjamin Mehorner, Oct. 24, 1790.
B. Grace, dau. of William and Mary Wilford, Aug. 7, 1723.
D. Grace, dau. of William and Mary Wilford, Aug. 30, 1723.
D. William Wilford, Nov. 13, 1726.
B. Grace dau. of William and Mary Wilford, Apr. 29, 1727.

D. Mary Wilford, July 24, 1738.
M. Mary Wilkerson and James Jones, Apr. 6, 1786.
M. John Wilkinson and Sarah Ross, Nov. 13, 1730.
B. William, son of John and Sarah Wilkinson, Oct. 14, 1731.
B. John, son of John and Sarah Wilkinson, Feb. 20, 1733/4.
D. Sarah Wilkinson, Mar. 3, 1733/4.
M. Samuel Wilkinson and Mary Cotes, Dec. 9, 1734.
M. John Wilkinson and Katherine Copley, Aug. 14, 1743.
B. Barnaby, son of William and Helena Williams, Mar. 10, 1716/7 and baptized
      Mar. 31, 1717.
B. Thomas, son of Thomas and Sarah Williams, dec'd., Feb. 15, 1717/8.
D. Sarah, wife of Thomas Williams, Apr. 22, 1718.
B. Jacob Williams, May 5, 1723.
M. Thomas Williams and Helen Murphy, Sept. 4, 1723.
D. Helena (Helen?) Williams, Oct. 6, 1725.
M. Sarah Williams and Bryant Handley, Dec. 28, 1726.
M. Frances Williams and Paul Sweeny, Dec. 24, 1728.
M. George Williams and Alice Fowler of Brunswick Parish, Dec. 31, 1734.
M. Anne Williams and John Bateman, Feb. 4, 1740/1.
B. Elizabeth, dau. of Alexander and Anne Williams, Mar. 10, 1742/3.
M. William Williams and Mildred Duncomb, Dec. 8, 1743.
M. Thomas Williams and Janet Johnson, Nov. 13, 1744.
M. Thomas Williams and Anne Floyd, Dec. 23, 1744.
B. John, son of Alexander and Anne Williams, Feb. 1, 1745/6.
B. John, son of John and Mary Williams, Jan. 22, 1746/7.
M. Jacob Williams and Elizabeth Miller, Dec. 3, 1747.
B. James, son of James and Elizabeth Williams, Jan. 11, 1774.
M. James Williams and Molly Price, Apr. 24, 1782.
M. Walter Williamson and Mildred Dade, Mar. 1, 1755.
B. Margaret, dau. of Walter and Mildred Williamson, Oct. 6, 1755.
B. Walter, son of Walter and Mildred Williamson, Nov. 13, 1758.
B. Mildred, dau. of Walter and Mildred Williamson, Apr. 3, 1762.
D. Margaret, dau. of Walter and Mildred Williamson, Nov. 18, 1837. (?)
M. John Willis and Elizabeth Plunket of Hanover Parish, Jan. 17, 1734/5.
B. William, son of Joan Willis, Feb. 22, 1742/3.
M. Anne Willis and James Ward, June 29, 1777.
M. Richard Wilson and Anne Smith, Oct. 31, 1722.
B. William, son of Thomas and Anne Wilson, June 7, 1726.
B. John, son of Richard and Anne Wilson, Nov. 11, 1726.
B. Anne, dau. of Richard and Elizabeth Wilson, Jan. 30, 1736/7.
B. John, son of John and Anne Wilson, Feb. 12, 1738/9.
B. Richard, son of Richard and Elizabeth Wilson, Sept. 7, 1739.
B. Thomas, son of Richard and Elizabeth Wilson, Oct. 21, 1744.
M. John Wilson and Jane Wood, Feb. 12, 1750/1.
M. Benjamin Wilson and Alinda McDonald, Feb. 27, 1757.
B. Andrew, son of Benjamin and Alinda Wilson, Dec. 14, 1757.
M. John Wilson and Anne Lambert, Oct. 28, 1759.
B. Mary, dau. of Benjamin and Eleanor (Alinda?) Wilson, Sept. 21, 1760.
B. Francis, son of William and Catherine Wilson, Oct. 7, 1772.
M. Nelly Wilson and William Lord, Apr. 7, 1780.
M. Catherine Wilson and Aaron Owens, Mar. 26, 1785.
M. Mary Wilton and Carnaby Peyton, July 5, 1764.
M. William Winters and Caty Hooe, Nov. 1, 1781.
M. Lettice Woaker (Walker?) and John Duncan, Sept. 27, 1735.
M. Elijah Wood and Jane Powell, June 20, 1722.
B. Mary, dau. of Elijah and Jane Wood, June 11, 1727.

D. Richard Wood, Nov. 23, 1729.
B. Jane, dau. of Elijah and Jane Wood, Jan. 28, 1730/1.
B. Sarah, dau. of Elijah and Jane Wood, Apr. 17, 1733.
D. Elijah Wood, Mar. 7, 1733/4.
D. Jane, widow of Elijah Wood, Mar. 11, 1733/4.
M. Jane Wood and Matthew Dyall, Jan. 23, 1738/9.
M. Mary Wood and Malcolm McIntosh, Nov. 24, 1743.
M. Jane Wood and John Wilson, Feb. 12, 1750/1.
D. Margaret Wooten, Jan. 24, 1725/6.
M. Sarah Worley and John Shotwell, June 26, 1725.
B. William, son of William and Sarah Worley, Mar. 30, 1761.
B. John, son of William and Mary Worrell, Sept. 2, 1737.
B. William, son of William and Mary Worrell, Aug. 13, 1740.
B. Mary, dau. of William and Mary Worrell, Apr. 19, 1743.
B. Philip, son of William and Mary Worrell, June 16, 1746.
M. Jacob Wray and Mary Ashton, May 13, 1761.
M. Helen Wray and Charles Stuart, Oct. 31, 1783.
M. Mary Wray and John Alexander Stuart, Nov. 17, 1785.
D. Mottram Wright, Nov. 26, 1729.
M. Francis Wright and Anne Massey, Dec. 7, 1737.
M. John Lee Wright and Mary Kitchen, Aug. 8, 1751.

Y

M. Elizabeth Yates and Robert Welch, Aug. 12, 1729.
M. James Yates of Sittenbourne Parish and Mary Green of Washington Parish,
    Nov. 19, 1745.
M. Robert Yates and Elizabeth Dade, Feb. 17, 1750/1.
B. Robert, son of Robert and Elizabeth Yates, July 22, 1752.
B. Henry, son of Robert and Elizabeth Yates, Jan. 10, 1754.
B. Charles, son of Robert and Elizabeth Yates, Aug. 5, 1756.
B. Henry Francis Dade, son of Robert and Elizabeth Yates, Aug. 20, 1765.
M. Robert Yates and Jane Dade, Apr. 11, 1777.
M. William Young and Elizabeth Griggs, Aug. 29, 1746.
B. William, son of William (and Elizabeth?) Young, Oct. 19, 1753.
B. Eleanor, dau. of William and Elizabeth Young, Mar. 2, 1757.
B. David, son of William and Elizabeth Young, Feb. 15, 1759.

Z

M. Thomas Zachary and Anne Griffin, Apr. 20, 1760.

PARTLY LEGIBLE ENTRIES:

B. Coldspring, dau. of William -------------- 1728.
B. Jane, dau. of William --------------------- 1728.
B. John, son of William and Elizabeth ------- 1728.

KING GEORGE COUNTY MARRIAGES

A list of some Marriage Licenses issued in King George county copied from Fee books kept by the County Clerk:

1768 -	Oct.	John Thomas and Jane Green
	Oct.	Aaron Potes and Ann Bruce
	Dec.	William Bankhead and Katy Vaulx
	Dec.	John Cox and Margaret Glendening
1769 -	Jan.	Gavin Lawson and Susannah Rose
	Sept.	James Triplett and Jenny Pearce
	Oct.	Joseph Murdock and Mary Tankersley
	Nov.	Mark Thorp and Susannah Stewart
1770 -	Jan.	Edward Dobbyns and Kay
	Feb.	Lawrence Balthrop and White
	Feb.	William Boon and Kezziah Greene
	Mar.	John Dukes and Mary Briscoe
	June	Richard Buckner and Jenny Riding
	June	Charles Burton and Jane Chapman
	June	John Grigsby and Elizabeth Robinson
	Dec.	Al. Thorn (Thom) and Sarah Triplett
1771 -	Feb.	John Payne and Susannah Ficklen
	Apr.	William Pitman and Catharine Pead
	Apr.	D. Fitzhugh and Alice Riden
	June	John Millett and Salley Suter
	Aug.	Henry Grigsby and Lucy Lang
	Nov. 15	John Spilman and Elizabeth Brown
	Nov.	John Kay and Caty Pead
	Nov.	James Benson and Dullibella Berry
	Dec.	James Shiglar and Mary Gaitskill
	Dec.	Richard Taylor and Catherine Davis
	Dec.	John Pollard and Mildred Skinker
	Dec.	Enoch Marshall and Nancy Green
	Dec.	Henry Smith and Mary Strother
	Dec.	James Armstrong and Mary Ann Henshaw
1772 -	Feb.	Thomas Steward and Elizabeth Hoomes
	Jan.	John Mazret (?) and Anne Wheeler
	Feb. 7	John Price and Ann Smith
	Feb.	William Thompson and Sarah Carter
	Mar.	Isaael Robinson and Sarah Riveley (?)
	Mar.	John Lurty and Rosey Bronaugh.
	Apr.	Aaron Thornley and Caty Dobyns
	Apr.	William Fewell and Anne Bell
	Apr.	Benjamin Pettit and Mary Banks
	Apr.	John Skinker and Peggy Vaulx
	Apr.	Simon Miller and Jane Hord
	May	William Butler and Rosey Courtney
	May	William Mills and Mildred Pollard
	May	Jessie Hord and Anky Hord
	May	George White and Suckey Drake
	June	John Simpson and Frances Sharpe
	July	William Smith and Anne Jacobs
	July	George Lunsford and Hester Lunsford
	Aug.	Henry Cliff and Elizabeth Smart
	Aug.	Rowley Smith and Billy Hord
	Aug.	Joseph Rogers and Mildred Jones

After Oct. 1772   John Sweatman and Sarah Ficklin
Oct. 1774 to
    Oct. 1775   Samuel Blackwell and Sarah Beale
               Benjamin Thomas and Caty Randall
               James Steward and Elizabeth Gaitskill
               John Sutor and Elizabeth Stringfellow
               Swanson Lunceford and Margaret Kerby Chesseldine
               Thomas Jett and Lusinah Owens. (Jan. 1775)
               George W. Spooner and Sally Drake
               Franklyn Syms and Sukey Drake
               Richard Todd and Elizabeth Davis
               William Spilman and Mary Brown
               James Ward and Jenny Jennings
               John Lovell and Ann Arnold

1776 - Oct.   Edward Moor and Helen McDonald
     Nov.   William Storke and Elizabeth Jett
     Nov.   Daniel Triplett and Elizabeth Richards
     Dec.   Winifred Eustice Beale and Hancock Lee
     Dec.   George Rankins and Judith Marshall

N O T E S

OPR means Overwharton Parish Register, Stafford Co., Va.

1. Alternative spelling, Findleston. See in alphabetical listing under "F".

2. Westmoreland Co., Va. Book 1721-1731, p. 68, shows that Archibald Allen married Penelope, widow of Peter Skinner of that county.

3. OPR. Jacob, son of John and Annie (sic) Allenthorpe, was baptized, Dec. 24, 1742.
Sarah Allenthorpe and William Price were married Aug. 8, 1748.

4. Thomas Ammon died in King George county in 1742. His widow, Sarah, administered upon his estate.

5. "Note that this child does not belong to this Parish, but desired by the Parents to be registered here, which occasions its being misplaced." David Stuart, Minister.

6. Pavier?

7. Stafford Co., Va. Book Z, p. 261, shows that William Balltrop married Margaret, daughter of Nathaniel Jones of Westmoreland County before March 30, 1705.

8. Joseph Berry died in King George Co., 1749/50. Joseph and Benj: Berry administered upon his estate.

9. Stafford Co., Va. Book P, p. 241, dated Nov. 5, 1759. Marriage contract between Capt. Zachariah Brazier and Mrs. Elizabeth Buckner, widow.

10. OPR. Priscilla, daughter of William Burton, born Jan. 17, 1745/6.
William Burton and Rachel Porch were married Oct. 7, 1753.
Samuel, son of Wm. and Rachel Burton, b. April 20, 1756.

11. OPR. George, son of George Bush, b. Aug. 10, 1748.
John, son of Geo. and Mary Bush, b. Dec. 10, 1751.
Elizabeth, dau. of George and Mary Bush, b. Feb. 20, 1758.

12. OPR. Peter, son of Peter and Charity Cash, b. July 17, 1746.
Elizabeth Cash mar. Calvert Porter, Sept. 21, 1749.
Elizabeth Cash, bapt. June 24, 1750.
Elizabeth Cash, died March 9, 1750/1.
Jean Cash, m. William Waters, April 6, 1751.
James, son of Peter and Charity Cash, b. Oct. 26, 1753.

13. OPR. Rawleigh Chinn and Sarah Lacy, m. Sept. 2, 1748.
Margaret, dau. of Rawleigh and Sarah Chinn, b. May 14, 1749.
Anne, dau. of Rawleigh Chinn, Jr. b. Jan. 15, 1754.

14. Alternative spellings: Crofford, Grafford, Crawford.

15. After this entry appears the following: "Note that several of the above children's names are wrong inserted as to the year of God, by reason of the carelessness of the Clerk, which occasioned me taking the Register into my own Care and Management." (signed) David Stuart, Minister.

16. OPR. Mary, dau. of William Eaton, b. May 22, 1744.
    Sarah, dau. of William Eaton, b. Sept. 20, 1747.

17. Other spellings: Englis, Ingles, Cangles, etc.

18. William Fitzhugh, son of John and Anna Barbara Fitzhugh, was baptized on May 14, 1725. God Fathers: Colonel John Tayloe and Daniel McCarty. God Mothers: Madam Sarah McCarty and Winwood (sic) McCarty. Westmoreland Co., Va. Book V. p. 510 shows that "John Fitzhugh of Stafford County, Gent." married Anna Barbara, the eldest daughter of Daniel McCarty, Gent., of Westmoreland county before or about Dec. 5, 1715.

19. Lancaster County Marriage Bonds:
    Henry Fitzhugh of Stafford county and Lucy, daughter of Robert Carter, who gave his consent on July 28, 1730.

20. The will of William Beverley of "Blandfield," Essex County, probated 3 May, 1756, mentioned his daughter, Ursula Fitzhugh.

21. Stafford County, Book O, p. 112, shows that (James) Fletcher had married Rachel Sebastian, administratrix of Isaac Sebastian, before July 11, 1750.

22. OPR. William Chandler, son of Chandler and Mary Fowke, b. Sept. 4, 1720.
    John, son of same, b. Jan. 17, 1724/5.
    Elizabeth, daughter of same, b. April 27, 1727.
    Chandler, son of same, b. Sept. 3, 1732.
    Anne, dau. of same, d. Dec. 8, 1732.
    Sarah, dau. of same, b. Aug. 10, 1734.
    Anne, dau. of same, b. Sept. 4, 1737.
    Sarah, dau. of same, d. Oct. 14, 1739.
    Susannah, dau. of same, b. Oct. 24, 1739.
    John, son of same, d. April, 16, 1740.
    Richard, son of same, b. Nov. 11, 1741.
    William Fowke, d. Oct. 24, 1742.
    William, son of Chandler and Mary Fowke, b. May 31, 1743.
    William, son of same, d. Dec. 2, 1743.
    Capt. Chandler Fowke of Gunstan Hall, in Stafford County, d. Feb. 10, 1744/5.
    Gerard Fowke and Elizabeth Dinwiddie m. Nov. 26, 1745.
    Fauquier County Marriages:
    Chandler Fowke and Mary Harrison, Dec. 19, 1759.

23. John Franklin died in King George county in 1724. George Franklin was the executor of his will.

24. Stafford County, Book M, p. 249, shows that Martha, widow of Nicholas George, married Thomas Drummond before Oct. 13, 1737.

25. Stafford County, Book O, pp. 244, 464, shows that "Mr. George Gray" married Mary, sister of James Strother.

26. King George County, Book 1, p. 617. Thomas Grigsby of Stafford County and his wife, Rose Newton, daughter of Garrard Newton, late of Richmond county, were married before Oct. 3, 1729.

27. OPR. Sarah Grigsby and William Ross m. June 5, 1753.
    Moses Grigsby and Mary Matheny m. Aug. 26, 1753.

28. Fairfax County, Will Book C, p. 9, shows that the estate of Futural Hall was inventoried by Ann Hall, his admx:, Aug. 19, 1767.

29. OPR. William, son of Peter and Margaret Hedgman, b. July 1, 1732.
    John, son of same, b. Oct. 13, 1741.
    Margaret, wife of Peter Hedgman, d. Jan. 16, 1754.
    George Hedgman and Hannah Daniel m. Nov. 27, 1756.

30. Rice, son of Rice and Katherine Hooe, was bapt. May 6, 1725. God Fathers: Cadwallader Dade and John Hooe. God Mother: Sarah Hooe.

31. Gerrard Hooe married Sarah Barnes, Jan. 9, 1761, Richmond County Marriage Licenses; Thomas Barnes, security.

32. OPR. Franky, dau. of William and Sarah Humphreys, b. March 8, 1755.

33. King George County, Book L, p. 467, shows a John James m. Anne, dau. of James Trent, before 1, Dec. 1727.
    Stafford County, Book M, p. 309, shows a John James m. Dinah, dau. of William Allen, bef. 16 Aug. 1738.

34. No attempt has been made to distinguish between Johnson and Johnston.

35. Henry Jones died in King George County in 1735. Anne Jones, his widow, administered upon his estate.

36. Stafford County, Book M, p. 244, shows that Edmund Kelly m. Jane, widow of George Griggs, before July 12, 1737.

37. OPR. Sarah Kelly and William Sebastian were married June 11, 1751.

38. Peter Kerr died in King George County in 1736. Sarah Kerr, his widow, administered upon his estate.

39. John Knight of Stafford County married Catherine Philips of Richmond County in June, 1715, according to the Register of Farnham Parish.

40. OPR. Sarah Lacy and Rawleigh Chinn were married Sept. 2, 1748.

41. The will of Edward Layer (sic), deceased, was filed in Stafford County in 1740.

42. Henry Locke died in King George County in 1738. Elizabeth Locke, his widow, resigned her executorship and William Thornton acted in her stead.

43. Order Book 1, p. 120 of King George County and Deed Book 8, part 1, p. 52, Westmoreland County, show that Daniel McCarty married Anne, widow of William Fitzhugh, Esq., before May 3, 1723. Capt. Daniel McCarty (1679-1724) was of Cople Parish, Westmoreland County. Anne was the dau. of

Richard and Lettice (Corbin) Lee of Stratford. Col. Wm. Fitzhugh was of "Eagle's Nest," a son of the immigrant William Fitzhugh.

44. Mannan was an alternative spelling.

45. Prince William County, Land Causes, p. 96, shows that Dade Massey married Parthenia, dau. of Robert Alexander, before April 28, 1735.

46. OPR. Thomas Massey and Eleanor Perender (sic) were married June 26, 1745. (He seems to have married secondly or thirdly Eleanor Bunbury of King George County, as she is named in the will of her father, Thomas Bunbury, probated in 1779. The will of Thomas Massey was probated in the same county the preceding year.)

47. OPR. Triplett, son of Slvester and Elizabeth Moss, born Aug. 9, 1752.

48. King George County, Order Book, shows that John Naylor died June 8, 1735 and that John Simpson married his daughter.

49. Peter Nugent died in King George County in 1750. John Elkins administered upon his estate.

50. King George County, Book 3, p. 175, shows that Anthony Peyton married Anne Carnaby, dau. of Anthony Carnaby of Hanover Parish, before Sept. 26, 1746. Carnaby Peyton was doubtless their son.

51. OPR. Stephen Pilcher married Lucy Clarke, Nov. 7, 1748.
Samuel, son of Stephen and Lucy Pilcher, b. Jan. 5, 1749/50.
Elizabeth Pilcher, d. Jan. 23, 1749/50.
James, son of Stephen Pilcher, was born Feb. 17, 1749/50.
Stephen Pilcher m. Bridget McConchie, Dec. 1, 1750.
(William McConchie m. Bridget Whitecotton, Nov. 10, 1747. George White-cotton died March 23, 1743/4, leaving a widow Bridget.)
Mary Pilcher died at Alexander McCantee's, Jan. 25, 1754.

52. OPR. Thomas Porter d. Feb. 26, 1738/40.
Calvert Porter m. Elizabeth Cash, Sept. 21, 1749.
Joseph, son of Calvert and Elizabeth Porter, b. Oct. 21, 1749 (?1750)
Calvert, son of same, b. March 1, 1752.
Thomas, son of same, b. Jan. 11, 1754.
John Porter died July 14, 1754.
Frances, dau. of Calvert and Elizabeth Porter, b. Jan. 12, 1756.
Thomas Porter was baptized, Feb. 23, 1756.
Joseph Porter m. Jemima Smith, Feb. 24, 1756.
Charity, dau. of Calvert and Elizabeth Porter, b. Sept. 9, 1757.

53. OPR. William Price and Sarah Allenthorpe were married, Aug. 8, 1748.

54. OPR. Jean, dau. of Robert Reddish, b. Jan. 8, 1740/1.

55. Alternative spelling Redish, Raddish, Radish.

56. OPR. Bridget Riggins and John Fliter m. March 16, 1755.

57. OPR. William Rose m. Sarah Grigsby, June 5, 1753.

58. Stafford County, Book M, p. 238, shows that (Nicholas) Savin had married Mary Moss, administratrix of John Moss, before April 13, 1737.

59. OPR. William Sebastian and Sarah Kelly were married June 11, 1751.

60. King George County, Order Book 1, p. 44, shows that John Simpson had married Elizabeth, dau. of John Naylor, before Dec. 6, 1735.

61. OPR. Enoch, son of John and Rosamond Spinks, b. Nov. 10, 1742.

62. OPR. Josias, son of Josias and Mary Stone, b. June 17, 1747.

63. Widow of William Storke (1690-1726) and daughter of Edward and Margaret Hart of Stafford County.

64. John Storke died Sept. 1, 1757, apparently in Westmoreland County. His wife Frances survived him.

65. An attempt has been made to distinguish between Stribling and Stripling. Probably the attempt was unnecessary!

66. OPR. Moses, son of Joseph and Jemima Sudduth, b. July 28, 1753. Sarah, dau. of Joseph Sudduth, bapt. April 13, 1756.

67. Alternative spelling Suddarth and Southard.

68. OPR. William Thornberry and Elizabeth O'Daniel m. July 10, 1746. Anne, dau. of Wm. and Elizabeth Thornberry, b. April 9, 1747.

69. Stafford County, Book M. p. 165, shows that a Richard Todd m. Lucy, sister of Charles Ellitt, Jr., before Sept. 29, 1734.

70. Joseph Tucker d. in King George County in 1735/6. Rosamond Tucker, his widow, administered upon his estate.

71. Alternative spelling Vinson.

72. Stafford County, Book M, p. 172, shows that John Washington had married Mary, dau. of Dade Massey (Sr.), long before April 16, 1735.

73. OPR. Bailey, son of Bailey and Catherine Washington, b. Dec. 12, 1753. John, son of same, b. May 5, 1756. Elizabeth, dau. of same, b. March 16, 1758.

74. The celebrated Revolutionary General.

75. OPR. Charles, son of Charles and Mary Wells, b. Jan. 10, 1739/40. John, son of same, b. July 3, 1742. Peyton, son of Charles Wells, b. Sept. 9, 1744. Eleanor, dau. of same, b. April 19, 1747. Benjamin, son of Charles and Mary Wells, b. Aug. 22, 1751.